Enhancing The Prophetic In You

Kimberly Moses

Copyright © 2018 by Kimberly Moses

All rights reserved
Rejoice Essential Publishing
P.O. BOX 512
Effingham, SC 29541

www.republishing.org

All rights reserved. No part of this book may be used or reproduced by any means, graphic, electronic, or mechanical, including photocopying, recording, taping or by any information storage retrieval system without the written permission of the publisher except in the case of brief quotations embodied in critical articles and reviews.

Scripture quotations taken from the New American Standard Bible® (NASB), Copyright © 1960, 1962, 1963, 1968, 1971, 1972, 1973, 1975, 1977, 1995 by The Lockman Foundation Used by permission. www.Lockman.org

Scripture quotations taken from the Amplified® Bible (AMP), Copyright © 2015 by The Lockman Foundation Used by permission. www.Lockman.org"

Unless otherwise indicated, Scripture is taken from the King James Version

Visit the author's website at www.prophetessk.org

Enhancing The Prophetic In You/ Kimberly Moses

ISBN-10: 1-946756-22-9
ISBN-13: 978-1-946756-22-0

Library of Congress Control Number: 2018934527

DEDICATION

I dedicate this book to everyone that supports my ministry and to all my students; past, current, and future. Thank you Keiyia Jackson-George for everything that you have done to help improve my writing. Thank you, Pastor Kevin B. Brewer for going above and beyond to encourage me to continue writing. Thank you Tron Moses for supporting me and always having the right words of encouragement. I am thankful for my children, Moriah and Lamont Jr.

Table Of Contents

Acknowledgment……………………………………xi

Endorsement…………………………………………xii

Unit One: Laying The Foundation………………xvi

Introduction……………………………………………1

Enhancing Exercises…………………………………4

Prayers For God to Fill Our Mouths……………18

What Is Prophetic Ministry………………………26

Prophetic Protocol…………………………………30

The Do's of Prophecy………………………………36

The Don'ts of Prophecy……………………………45

Prophets and the Other Five-Fold………………50

Effective Prophetic Ministry………………………56

Unit Two: Different Ways God Speaks…………71

Prophetic Vehicles …………………………………72

External Voice………………………………………76

Internal Voice of God..................................83

Prophets..89

Talking Unaware.......................................93

Reaffirmation...95

Dreams and Visions..................................98

Perception..104

Preaching...107

Proxy...110

Writing..112

Parables...117

Prophetic Action....................................125

Sealing the word....................................129

Prayer...131

Angels...134

The Scriptures......................................139

Unit Three: True Characteristic Of A Prophet..143

Characteristics Of A True Prophet Of God.....144

Love..149

Joy..154

Peace..157

- Longsuffering...160
- Gentleness..164
- Goodness..167
- Faithful...169
- Meekness..172
- Temperance..175
- Brokenness...179
- Humility...182
- Servants...185
- Faith Filled..188
- Courageous...191
- Wise...194
- Spirit Led..198
- Obedient To God......................................202
- Integrity..205
- Compassion..208
- Commitment..211
- Righteousness..214
- Surrendered...216

ACKNOWLEDGEMENTS

This book wouldn't be possible without the inspiration of the Holy Spirit. He gave me the blueprint and I just obeyed as I wrote the manuscript. He said that this book will change my life. I am excited to see the fruition of those words.

2 Timothy 3:16-17 says, "All scripture is given by inspiration of God, and is profitable for doctrine, for reproof, for correction, for instruction in righteousness: That the man of God may be perfect, thoroughly furnished unto all good works."

Enhancing the Prophetic is a book that will bring you to a place of peace, transparency, and clarity on how to operate in the prophetic anointing God has placed over your life. As God speaks to His children, He desires them to grow daily in wisdom and revelation of His voice and His attributes. This book will definitely provide you with the golden keys you need to unlock the spiritual gate of enhancing the understanding of how to flow into the prophetic and hearing the voice of God clearly. You will begin to operate in the way He desires for you to move in the earth.

Prophetess Kimberly Moses is a very humble and astonishing woman of God. She has established a powerful prophetic ministry with a healing and deliverance anointing. Truly she is a gift to the body of Christ. Her books such as Set the Captives Free and Empowering the New Me have such revelation that is timeless and will transform every reader. Her books bring wisdom and revelation and empower believers to walk in their divine purpose and to achieve their goals to be all that God called them to be.

Kim has the ability to transform people's mind and bring them into a place to be more intimate with God. Truly anyone that reads her books will receive knowledge, understanding, and revelation. They will also be able to receive impartation of the prophetic grace that is upon her life. This powerful woman of God has blessed many across the world. She has a passion to see people saved and set free. She has developed a strong relationship with the Lord Jesus Christ, and her zeal for God comes from a modest, pure place. Even I have been blessed by her ministry. She has been a great friend and has also released prophetic words over my life that have come to pass. Truly, THIS woman is a contribution to the body of Christ and I am so honored to know her as a prophetess and, most of all, as a friend! Much more grace and favor be upon each one of you in the name of Jesus.

Prophet Timothy Long
Timothy Long Ministries

Unit One

Laying The Foundation

CHAPTER ONE
Introduction

Many people can hear from God but desire to hear from Him more. They desire to have increased or heighten senses in the realm of the spirit. The word enhance means heighten, increase; especially :to increase or improve in value, quality, desirability, or attractiveness.[1] Mature saints have a hunger that is insatiable to grow in God.

Matthew 5:6 says, "Blessed are they which do hunger and thirst after righteousness: for they shall be filled."

They aren't satisfied with being used one time. They want God to use them continually.

Psalm 63:1 says, "O God, thou art my God; early will I seek thee: my soul thirsteth for thee, my flesh longeth for thee in a dry and thirsty land, where no water is;"

They want to live in the vine and stay in the flow. You may be able to prophesy accurately, but what about prophesying with deeper revelation? What about receiving more information when you prophesy? You can tell how seasoned or how much a prophet ranks in the spirit by the revelation of their prophecies.

I am not satisfied with basic level prophecy such as, "God is going to bless you." I want to know the secrets of men's hearts so I can intercede for them more effectively. When God called me as a prophet, I decided to go all the way. I had no prior knowledge of what a prophet was. I had no prophetic training like the prophet Amos stated (Amos 7:14). There was just an overwhelming passion to excel at whom God called me to be. There is an unquenchable yearning inside me to always be in a state of receiving from God. I don't want heighten senses for my sake, I want it for God's Glory.

I want people to know that there was a prophet among them when I show up. I want people to know that God is real. I always say, "God, you called me. I didn't call myself. Therefore, I know that you will equip me with everything I need." I vowed before God to always put myself in a position to receive from him. There are several ways that will be discussed that can increase the prophetic revelation in our lives. We need to grow in grace and the knowledge of our Lord and Savior Jesus Christ (2 Peter 3:18). Whatever gift inside you that has been dormant is about to be unlocked. This will provoke you to seek God and enhance the prophetic in you!

CHAPTER TWO

Enhancing Exercises

1. ALONE TIME

Whenever we spend alone time with God, we are getting to know him. Think of yourself like you are in a relationship with God. A covenant relationship. If you are married, you spend time with your spouse to be intimate. If you are in a courtship, you are spending time with your potential spouse to get to know them. Time is valuable, and it's something we can't get back. Spending time with God is one way to have prophetic accuracy. For three years, I was away from my family in Colorado. I spend a lot of time with God. I would lock myself in my apartment and talk with him throughout my day. I was lonely, and I found comfort in Him (John 14:26). Abraham, who was a prophet, spent all day talking with God (Genesis 15). It is possible to spend time with God.

Many people have different livelihoods. However, you can bring the spirit of the Lord with you on your job. When I worked at the hospital years ago as a Respiratory Therapist, I brought God with me. People were aware that there was a woman of God in their midst. I would talk to God under my breath when I was walking down the hall. I would hear Him speak to me throughout my shift. I told God that I needed him to be with me always. He whispered back to me and told me every day for months that He was with me and would never leave me (Deuteronomy 31:6). When I am cooking dinner for my family or cleaning up my home, I am spending time with God. He has my focus. Many people have families so they feel like that can't spend as much time with God. It's all about balance. You have to make it work. You have to put in time and effort. In my old apartment, I spent hours in the bathtub speaking with God. There were certain areas in my apartment where God would meet me. He would speak to me on my old elliptical machine when I would work out in the mornings.

If you want to enhance the prophetic in your life, spending alone time with God is vital. Turn off the television and phone. I went years without watching television. All I wanted was God. Put the children to bed early if you have too. Tell your spouse, family, and friends that you have an important meeting. You have an important meeting with the Holy Spirit. They may not always understand but you have to get what you need from God.

- Write down some times throughout your day that you can spend alone with God. It could be on your way to work or early in the morning. Be creative. Make a commitment to God and keep it.

2. FASTING TIME

The Holy Spirit gave me instructions when He called me. He instructed me to fast one day per week. He deals with every person differently. I meet some prophets where they were instructed to fast one week out of the month or the first three days of each month. The point is, we are called to live a fasted lifestyle. Many people's stomachs are their gods. They aren't willing to push the plate of food to the side and seek after the things of the spirit. If you want to be empty of yourself and kill your flesh, then fasting is a must. When I fast, many miracles occur. One of the first times I did a three fast, God opened deaf ears when I prayed.

When I fasted twenty-one days, a lady was healed of scoliosis. Fasting allows you to operate in God's power. Jesus fasted forty days before He officially began His powerful ministry (Luke 4). God placed on various prophet's hearts to fast: David (Psalm 69:10), Jesus (Luke 4:2), Nehemiah (Nehemiah 1:4), Daniel (Daniel 9:3), Moses (Exodus 34:28), and John (Mark 2:18). They even proclaimed fasts (Joel 2:12; Isaiah 58). Fasting enhances the prophetic in our lives because it heightens our ability to hear God's voice. Whenever, I feel like I need to hear God clearly,

I fast. I shut the world out and proclaim a fast.

Whenever you fast, you have to put time in with prayer. This is the time to war with your prophecies (1 Timothy 1:18). I pray out every prophecy that I have received. I remind God of His promises. It takes work but the results are phenomenal. Bring your flesh underneath subjection and allow God's spirit to reign in your life. Make a commitment to live a fasted lifestyle. This means fast on a regular basis.

• Pray and ask Holy Spirit when you should fast. Also ask Him what type of fast you should do. Make an effort to obey the instructions that you hear. (Remember fasts in the bible were from food only. Abstaining from television or social media while eating food is not a biblical fast).

3. PRAYER TIME

I always ask the question, "How can you be a prophet and not pray?" Prayer is the time where you receive from God. Prophets are constantly pouring out but we have to spend time with God so He can pour back into us. For a season, my prayer time was 9 p.m. every night. The Lord spoke to me most of this time. I have many notebooks full of words that I received in my prayer time. Because I was consistent in my prayer time, the Lord would seek me at this time every night. If I was late, He would put impressions on my body with His fire. His fire would feel so sharp sometimes that I'd cried out and immediately went into prayer. Other times, the presence of the Lord will be strong around this time. It took time for me to build up this relationship with God.

I recall rushing home after church services or after work just to lay down on my face in my favorite spot in the living room. I couldn't wait to spend alone time with God. I knew God would tell me something that I didn't know or share with me what was on His heart. He would give me assignments where I had to intercede for people. He would even give me instructions for my next season. We see a pattern throughout the scriptures where prophets prayed: Abraham (Genesis 20:17), Moses (Numbers 11:2), Joel (Joel 2), Habakkuk (Habakkuk 3), Jesus (Mark 1:35), and so on. Prayer is part of the prophet's DNA.

There are different types of prayers and different ways to pray. However, we have to be led by God on how to pray effectively. We have to ensure that we build up our spirit man by praying in our heavenly language (Jude 20). Praying in tongues at least one hour minimum a day keeps me sharp and accurate in the prophetic. Don't miss out on your prayer time. Most of a prophet's ministry is spent behind closed doors praying.

• How can you be more consistent in your prayer time? What are the best times when you can pray?

4.. MEDITATION TIME

Meditation is vital. It's how we get the word of God embedded within our hearts. It's how we hear His voice through the word as we reflect on the scriptures. Taking the time to meditate on God's word is equipping us to fight with the sword of spirit (Ephesians 6:17). Meditation will allow us to be a sharpshooter in the realm of the spirit. When the enemy tries to attack us with demonic thoughts, we can easily counteract them with the word of God that was implanted within us when we took the time to meditate. There is nothing worse than stumbling and flipping through bible pages trying to figure out what to pray against the enemy during an attack. We should already have been students of the word of God by having the word of God within us.

One day, the Lord convicted me. He said, "You lost the art of meditation." He was right. For a season, I didn't meditate. Since then, I've made a conscious effort to do so. I would wake up early and pick one verse out of the bible. I would go over this verse all throughout the day. I would say it over again out loud until I knew it by heart. It was so supernatural because as soon as I would open my bible, the presence of the Lord would be really strong. I noticed over time when I began to prophesy, I would prophesy these bible verses at the right time when it was needed. The Holy Spirit brought these scriptures to my remembrance. My endurance in the prophetic increased as well. Once, I prophesied for six hours straight. I would've kept going if there were more people to prophesy over. Every scripture that I took time to place inside me by meditation just flowed out of me. Meditation is a powerful way to enhance the prophetic in you!

- How often do you meditate? Pick a bible verse every day and meditate on it. You can sign up for various bible apps that send a verse of the day. Write down scriptures that you have meditated on in a notebook.

5. WORSHIP TIME

Prophets love to worship. Worship attracts the presence of God. Every day, I lift up my hands and worship. Worship is loving on God and ministering to him. There were prophets that were appointed to worship God in the scriptures. They kept His presence strong in the atmosphere. Asaph worshipped before the ark of the covenant (1 Chronicles 16:37). Anna worshipped in the temple (Luke 2:37).

The presence of God feels like fire. Initially, He set the offering on fire (Leviticus 6:13), and it's our jobs to keep it burning symbolically. We can keep the presence of God strong in our lives by consistent worship. Before I do events or prophetic miracle conferences/calls, I worship at least one hour minimum. I ask God to consume me with His fire. The fire of God comes and everyone who comes in contact with me can feel His fire. Remember, you can't take the people somewhere publicly that you have not been privately. Worship makes my job easier. The Glory manifests and people get healed. The prophetic flows. The prophet Elisha worshipped before he prophesied.

2 Kings 3:15 says, "But now bring me a minstrel. And it came to pass, when the minstrel played, that the hand of the LORD came upon him."

Imagine how effective you would be if you took the time to worship before you prophesied?

• When can you fit worship in with your schedule? Do you have a list of songs that are anointed to usher in the presence of God?

6. STUDY TIME

Prophets have to be students of the word of God. Many prophets can prophesy but they lack knowledge of biblical prophets. I grew by leaps and bounds by studying the prophets of the bible. Every week, I have a series that comes on my social media platforms called "The Making of a Prophet." I examine each prophet's life and try to find the relatability to strengthen my own life. I have learned many errors and have seen patterns on what to do and what not to do. Studying the prophets and other scriptures created a great foundation of the word in my life. It has also opened many doors and opportunities that I am able to equip the body of Christ. I made a commitment to be the best prophet of God that I could be when God called me.

2 Timothy 2:15 says, "Study to shew thyself approved unto God, a workman that needeth not to be ashamed, rightly dividing the word of truth."

I have often invested in classes and trainings to receive revelation of things that I didn't know in the word of God. Remember, if the enemy knows the word then God's children should too. Satan knew scriptures when he tempted

Jesus in the wilderness (Luke 4). I refuse to allow a witch to outdo me in the spirit. I refuse to allow the enemy to know more word than I do. Let's take the time and study the word. Studying the word will ensure that your prophecies are lining up with scriptures. You never want to prophesy something that is contrary to the word of God. Are you a student of the word?

• When can you incorporate studying the scriptures in your daily routine? Have you invested in classes, training, workbooks, or study bibles? (Great job for getting this book. You made a spiritual investment).

7. STEPPING OUT IN FAITH

When I stepped out in faith and spoke what I saw or heard, then God gave me more. I had no idea if the word made sense or not. I just knew that I had been spending time with God, so what I was perceiving was from Him. The more I released what I got, the more I received. God was using me to build what seemed like pieces to a puzzle.

1 Corinthians 13:9 says, "For we know in part, and we prophesy in part."

Amazingly, the recipient testified how accurate the prophetic word was. Prophets have to have faith to prophesy. As we go through trials, our faith in God is increased. God wants to get us to the point where we open up our mouths and He just fills it. When you step out in faith, there is no time for holding back. You are allowing the Holy Spirit to have His way through you.

Years ago, I had anxiety, and it hindered me from doing so many things. As I grew in God, trusted him, my faith increased and the fear diminished. I wrote a book called, "Walk by Faith: A Daily Devotional." I give testimonies of how I have had to have faith in trying times. Remember, fear will block the area where faith needs to be. Faith has to be present in order for God to truly move in our lives. God will not lead you astray as you obey him and step out in faith.

• What ways can you step out in faith? Are you obeying everything that God has told you to do?

8. COMPANY OF PROPHETS

Being around other prophets will sharpen your gift.

Proverbs 27:17 says, "Iron sharpeneth iron; so a man sharpeneth the countenance of his friend."

We see a pattern in the word of God where prophets hung around other prophets (2 Kings 2:3; 4:38; 5:22). I won't spend too much time talking about this subject because I discuss this in great detail in "School Of The Prophets: A Curriculum for Success." All of my friends are prophetic. We strengthen each other. If you want to grow in your gift, get around and stay around the prophetic anointing.

• Do you have any prophets in your life that are able to train you and keep you active in your gift?

CHAPTER THREE

Prayers For God to Fill Our Mouths

One way that I always have the word of the Lord in my mouth is by praying the following prayers. The Lord often fills my mouth with his word. I step out in faith. My natural mind is cut off. I don't see anything. Most of the time, I don't hear anything. However, I am feeling the unction of the Holy Spirit. When I am in His presence, he seizes me just like he did prophet Ezekiel. He fills me with His spirit and speaks through me. Often times, the words out of my mouth bypass my mind. I am shocked at what's coming out of my mouth because it's the Lord speaking through me. People always come back and testify at how accurate the word of the Lord is out of my mouth. Praying for God to fill my mouth changed my life and it will change yours.

Then the Lord put forth his hand, and touched my mouth. And the Lord said unto me, Behold, I have put my words in thy mouth (Jeremiah 1:9).

You are the God that has made my mouth. Thank you, O Lord for placing your word in my mouth (Exodus 4:11).

Then I will go and you will be with my mouth, and teach me what I am to say (Exodus 4:12).

Lord, teach me what to do and what to say always in Jesus' name.

Lord, put a word in my mouth for your people in Jesus name.

I decree that God will raise up a prophet from among his people, like me, and put his words in my mouth. I shall speak to them all that God has commanded me (Deuteronomy 18:18).

I decree that God has touched my mouth with it and said, "Behold, this has touched your lips; and your iniquity is taken away and your sin is forgiven (Isaiah 6:7)."

I decree that God has put His words in my mouth and has covered me with the shadow of His hand, to establish the heavens, to found the earth, and to say to Zion, 'You are My people' (Isaiah 51:16).

I decree that your word will be like fire in my mouth (Jeremiah 5:14).

And he hath made my mouth like a sharp sword; in the shadow of his hand hath he hid me, and made me a polished shaft; in his quiver hath he hid me (Isaiah 49:2).

The Lord GOD hath given me the tongue of the learned, that I should know how to speak a word in season to him that is weary: he wakeneth morning by morning, he wakeneth mine ear to hear as the learned (Isaiah 50:4).

I decree and declare that God will give me a mouth and wisdom, which all my adversaries shall not be able to gainsay nor resist (Luke 21:15).

I decree that all the words that you speak I will receive in my heart and hear with my ears (Ezekiel 3:10).

For the Holy Ghost shall teach me in the same hour what I ought to say (Luke 12:12).

I decree the word of God out of my mouth is quick, and powerful, and sharper than any two-edged sword, piercing even to the dividing asunder of soul and spirit, and of the joints and marrow, and is a discerner of the thoughts and intents of the heart (Hebrews 4:12).

I decree that I will wage war against the enemy with the sword of the Lord in my mouth.

My voice shalt thou hear in the morning, O Lord; in the morning will I direct my prayer unto thee, and will look up (Psalm 5:3).

But unto thee have I cried, O Lord; and in the morning shall my prayer prevent thee (Psalm 88:13).

I wake up early in the morning and get up before dawn. I cry out. I hope in your word (Psalm 119:147).

Cause me to hear thy lovingkindness in the morning; for in thee do I trust: cause me to know the way wherein I should walk; for I lift up my soul unto thee (Psalm 143:8)

Lord, open my mouth in the midst of your people so they know that you are God (Ezekiel 29:21).

Is not your word like as a fire? Like a hammer that breaks the rock in pieces (Jeremiah 23:29)?

I decree that the spirit of the Lord is upon me. His words will not depart from my mouth, nor from the mouth of my offspring, nor from the mouth of my offspring's offspring from now and forever (Isaiah 59:21).

I decree that I will prophesy with boldness in Jesus' name.

I decree that none of my words will fall to the ground in Jesus name.

I decree that I will prophesy with precision and accuracy in Jesus name.

I decree that I will open my mouth and you will fill it (Psalm 81:10)

With my lips have I declared all the judgments of thy mouth (Psalm 119:13).

I decree that I am a child of God and the word of the Lord in my mouth is true.

I decree that my mouth will be used as a slave of righteousness.

I decree that my mouth will not be defiled in Jesus name.

I decree that my mouth will be used for the Glory of God.

The mouth of a righteous man is a well of life: but violence covereth the mouth of the wicked (Proverbs 10:11).

Let the words of my mouth, and the meditation of my heart, be acceptable in thy sight, O Lord, my strength, and my redeemer (Psalm 19:14).

For my mouth shall speak truth; and wickedness is an abomination to my lips (Proverbs 8:7).

Let my mouth be filled with thy praise and with thy honour all the day (Psalm 71:8).

O Lord, open my lips, That my mouth may declare Your praise (NASB Psalm 51:15).

My soul shall be satisfied as with marrow and fatness; and my mouth shall praise thee with joyful lips (Psalm 63:5).

I will sing of the mercies of the Lord for ever: with my mouth will I make known thy faithfulness to all generations (Psalm 89:1).

My mouth shall tell of Your righteous acts and of Your deeds of salvation all the day, for their number is more than I know (AMP Psalm 71:15).

My mouth shall speak of wisdom; and the meditation of my heart shall be of understanding (Psalm 49:3).

The mouth of the righteous speaketh wisdom, and his tongue talketh of judgment (Psalm 37:30).

The mouth of the just bringeth forth wisdom: but the froward tongue shall be cut out (Proverbs 10:31).

The law of truth will be in my mouth, and iniquity will not found on my lips. I will walked with God in peace and equity, and will turn many away from iniquity (Malachi 2:6).

I will open my mouth in a parable: I will utter dark sayings of old (Psalm 78:2).

CHAPTER FOUR

What is Prophetic Ministry?

Many people lack the knowledge of what true prophetic ministry is. True prophetic ministry isn't a ministry that originates from flesh or the mind of men. True prophecy originates from the Holy Spirit. Too often we call an old word that was fresh last season prophetic. We call an old movement based on routines, rituals, and protocols prophetic. We quench the Holy Spirit from moving with tradition, blind religion, and by-laws. Sometimes the less a person knows the better. It is often best to have childlike faith to be more open to the move of the spirit. God is spontaneous at time. When the prophetic goes forth, sometimes, it is unpredictable. Therefore, we shouldn't limit God by trying to control how the spirit of God moves. We shouldn't cut off Holy Spirit from flowing by placing time restrictions.

WHAT IS PROPHETIC MINISTRY?

Prophetic ministry is any ministry that relies on the gift of prophecy and new revelation from God to guide the church to maturity.[2] This ministry involves receiving and releasing a rhema, or right now word, that the Holy Spirit gives. The word "rhema" has a Greek origin. It means what is said, word, or saying.[3] True prophetic ministry is about unlocking revelation and tapping into new realms of the Holy Spirit. True prophetic ministers help challenge the body of Christ by stirring up their spiritual gifts, provoking them to go higher in God, rebuking them for their sinful ways, and showing them how to get off spiritual milk to consuming spiritual meat. Prophetic ministers apply 1 Corinthians 14 verses 1 and 3. Let's look at 1 Corinthians 14:1 which says, "Follow after charity, and desire spiritual gifts, but rather that ye may prophesy."

Prophetic ministers aim for love. They have truly grasped the concept of 1 Corinthians 13 which talks about love being the greatest gift. These ministers want to operate in the supernatural and they are open to receive the gifts of the spirit. They take the time that needs to be invested to sharpen their prophetic gift.

Let's take a look at 1 Corinthians 14:3 which says, "But he that prophesieth speaketh unto men to edification, and exhortation, and comfort." I break down in great detail what edification, exhortation, and comfort mean in, "School Of The Prophets: A Curriculum For Success." Prophetic ministers don't have to be in prophetic office. They don't have to have titles in front of their name. They just flow in the basic realm of prophecy which is edification, exhortation, and comfort. Prophetic ministers realize that God's Spirit is the source of a strong prophetic ministry.

CHAPTER FIVE

Prophetic Protocol

You may notice that churches flow differently. For instance, some churches may allow prophecy to come forth after worship with an open mic. Other churches may allow anyone to get up and prophesy after the announcements. Some churches may only allow people who have gone through certain training or classes to flow as God is leading them. Each church has a protocol that they follow. Most leaders are protective over the members in the congregation so they will not allow visitors or just anyone to prophesy among them. That is understandable because they are spiritually responsible for the people that God has place under them to train up.

God is a God of order.

1 Corinthians 14:33 says, "For God is not the author of confusion, but of peace, as in all churches of the saints."

God has appointed the five-fold offices (Ephesians 4:11) to help bring order in the church. You may have an anointing to prophesy but there are certain protocols in every church that must be followed. You just can't walk into a random church and begin to prophesy. That's out of order. I have been in churches and had a word but didn't prophesy. The pastor didn't know me. I haven't been proven or tested to speak "Thus saith the Lord" in that church. So, I remained silent. However, God also gave that same exact word to someone else that was able to release it because the elders in that church gave the prophesier permission to release that word.

1 Corinthians 14:29-33 says, "And let two or three prophets speak, and let the others pass judgment. But if a revelation is made to another who is seated, let the first keep silent. For you can all prophesy one by one, so that all may learn and all may be exhorted; and the spirits of prophets are subject to prophets; for God is not a God of confusion but of peace, as in all the churches of the saints."

These scriptures are a great example of prophetic protocol. There could be 20 prophets in a room. It would be chaotic if all 20 of them were to start prophesying in a corporate setting. These scriptures help bring order. Let two or three prophets speak and everyone else judge the word.

Even if you did get a word, remain silent. If God wanted you to speak, trust me, he will provide an avenue for you to do so. This is about accountability and submission. There is a lack of submission today in the body of Christ. Some people want to do what they want to. They don't submit their ministry under someone else's that may be more seasoned or have more experience than them. This is why there is a lot of error and scandals in the body of Christ. God would be more pleased if you submit to the leaders in the church that you are attending than being a vessel of rebellion. If a person doesn't agree with everything concerning a particular church, then they should leave instead of causing division. Anything that is not with the vision of that house is division.

God called and appointed leaders.

Romans 13:1 says, "Let every person be in subjection to the governing authorities. For there is no authority except from God, and those which exist are established by God."

It doesn't matter if you don't like a particular person or agree with them. There still should be a level of respect for that individual. This even refers to secular people who are in certain political offices. We are called to pray for them, not to tear them down with our words.

Hebrews 13:17 says, "Obey your leaders, and submit to them for they keep watch over your souls, as those who will give an account. Let them do this with joy and not with grief, for this would be unprofitable for you."

You want your leaders to enjoy interceding for you. You don't want to grieve them. Most leaders are dealing with warfare that you may not even be aware of. When they are on the front line, the enemy is constantly throwing his darts at them. They appear to be strong and have everything together but they are flesh too. They have feelings too. They feel pain too. They have to give an account to God, not man, for your soul. God appointed leaders to pray for you and to train you. If a leader who carries the heart of God says you aren't ready to be released in ministry, then it's a great possibility that they are right.

Sometimes we may feel like our leaders are jealous of us or trying to hold us back. This isn't necessarily always the case. They may be trying to protect you or impart further revelation and gifts to you. Be patience. You will get your chance to prophesy. God will use you and will open doors at the right time. God is testing you to see how well he can trust you in the area of submission. Years ago, I had to sit still even though I had a word. I wrote down what I heard and later went to my leaders and asked for permission. They graciously allowed me to speak and to flow in my gifting. This didn't happen overnight. I had to be tested and tried. My leaders had to seek God about me. At the right time, God opened the door for me to prophesy and for my voice to be respected and heard.

CHAPTER SIX

The Do's of Prophecy

Apostle John Eckhardt wrote a book called, "God Still Speaks." Appendix B inside this book lists Prophetic Protocol[4]. The ideas of the Dos and Don'ts chapter inside this book have come from that book. I will just add my thoughts and build on the foundation he already laid. There is a right way and a wrong way to prophesy. We have to remain humble. This is expressing the true character of Jesus Christ. We will cover characteristic of a prophet of God in much detail in later chapters.

Whenever we are anointed, the miraculous will flow through us. Many people will be amazed and people will begin to hear about us. We have to remain humble because many doors will open. This is what happened with Jesus. His fame spread throughout the land (Matthew 9:26). We can't lose focus. It's about Jesus not us. Our identity should be in Christ. The miraculous things that God does through you is for His glory. As prophets, we have to stay in God's presence. Abiding in God's presence will help us not lose perspective. Humility will take us far.

Ephesians 4:2 says, "With all lowliness and meekness, with longsuffering, forbearing one another in love;"

As we bow down before the Lord, He will lift us up higher. Pride will cause destruction; it results in a loss of everything if there is no repentance.

Proverbs 16:18 says, "Pride goeth before destruction, and an haughty spirit before a fall."

King Nebuchadnezzar was very prideful. God had to humble him. He ate grass in the field like wild oxen for years and finally gave God the glory. He was blessed that God allowed him to get his kingdom back (Daniel 4).

We have to stay in our grace. In other words, stay in your lane or the area where you are the most efficient in. For instance, I am 100% confident when it comes to words of knowledge pertaining to the area of healing. I will get impressions on my body, feeling everything the person who needs healing is feeling. I also feel the fire of God in certain parts of my body and I know that God will heal that person of that infirmity. However, I am not always confident when it comes to receiving names or locations. I am more eager to step out and operate in healing than to give a word of knowledge about names. God graced me more in healing.

Romans 12:6 says, "Having then gifts differing according to the grace that is given to us, whether prophecy, let us prophesy according to the proportion of faith;"

I have received names before and they were accurate, but it doesn't happen on a regular basis compared to the healing impressions that I receive. I am believing God for a greater impartation to flow in the word of knowledge when it comes to receiving names. We have to be careful and make sure that it's God that we are receiving the information from. Staying in our grace helps protect others from receiving erroneous words and sanitizes the prophetic ministry. There are a lot of people who are lying on God. They are saying He said something that He never said. Be careful. Don't try to flow like someone else. Just be uniquely you.

We must die to self.

Galatians 2:20 says, "I am crucified with Christ: nevertheless I live; yet not I, but Christ liveth in me: and the life which I now live in the flesh I live by the faith of the Son of God, who loved me, and gave himself for me."

We must place our agendas on the backburner and pick up God's. We have to deny our flesh and walk in the spirit. Dying to self is a process and must be done daily. Prophets face a lot of rejection and if they aren't careful to allow God to heal them, then it can become dangerous. That prophet will then minister from a wounded place, hurting others in the process. For instance, the prophet may have been hurt in a relationship, and then goes around preaching every man is a cheater. That prophet is ministering from a wounded place or from their own spirit and not from the word of God.

Prophets must submit to leadership. We discussed submission briefly in the previous chapter. You are not your own. You can't do whatever you want to do. Your flesh may want to go out and fornicate or drink alcohol, however, you know that will grieve the Holy Spirit. Prophets have to be submitted to God and the leaders in their lives. Prophets have to hold God's word as their standard. They know that by submitting to their leaders they are actually submitting to God.

Colossians 3:23 says, "And whatsoever ye do, do it heartily, as to the Lord, and not unto men."

Your submission must come from a place for your reverence for God. Submitting to leadership means that if your leader tells you to sit down for a season, then that's what you have to do.

Prophets must remain teachable.

Proverbs 12:15 says, "The way of a fool is right in his own eyes: but he that hearkeneth unto counsel is wise."

I will be the first one to admit that I don't know everything. I am constantly learning. God is able to send great people in my life to bless me and to pour into me spiritually.

1 Peter 5:5 says, "Likewise, ye younger, submit yourselves unto the elder. Yea, all of you be subject one to another, and be clothed with humility: for God resisteth the proud, and giveth grace to the humble."

You may be anointed but lack wisdom in a particular area. God will allow you to have mentors, spiritual parents, or even peers who are able to provide guidance. Moses was very teachable. He loved God's people and gave so much of himself. His father-in-law, Jethro was able to give him great advice that prevented him from burning out (Exodus 18).

In the previous chapter, we discussed order. Prophets must flow with the order of service.

1 Corinthians 14:33 says, "For God is not the author of confusion, but of peace, as in all churches of the saints."

The Holy Spirit is spontaneous and He will lead the service if He is not quenched (1 Thessalonians 5:19). Prophets must know how to flow with the Holy Spirit. This takes time and will be mastered with a real relationship with God. For instance, you may want to preach from your notes, but the Holy Spirit may give you an urgency to stop and to begin to pray. Whenever we flow with the Holy Spirit our prophetic ministry will be more effective. Effective ministry will be discussed further in a later chapter.

It is not mandatory, but recommended, to use a recorder. Why? The answer is when you are flowing and prophesying, you will not remember everything that was spoken. God may use you to prophesy to forty people back to back. It's a high probability that you won't remember it all. Some people may approach you after service and ask, "What did you say again?" If you record it or have them record the prophecy on their phones as you are going forth, then you both can go back and review the word. Also recording the prophecy helps you have witnesses or a level of accountability to someone. I record every prophetic teleconference so people can go back over their word. If I forgot it, I can go back over it. If someone approaches me about it, I can further assist them.

Prophets must operate in love.

1 Corinthians 14:1 says, "Follow after charity, and desire spiritual gifts, but rather that ye may prophesy."

We have to remember that people are hurting and God loves them. Jesus did the miraculous because He loved people. He had compassion for them. The prophetic grace on our lives will be that much more effective, and we will reach a lot more people if we operate in love. People will be mean sometimes, but we can't take it personally. Jesus prayed for His crucifiers on the cross (Luke 23:34). How can you say that you love God but manifest hate and lack of compassion for God's people?

1 John 4:20 says, "If a man say, I love God, and hateth his brother, he is a liar: for he that loveth not his brother whom he hath seen, how can he love God whom he hath not seen?"

CHAPTER SEVEN

The Don'ts of Prophecy

Have you gotten a word that was too long and full of fluff? The first don'ts of prophecy is don't prophesy too long. You may be asking yourself, what is fluff? Fluff is full of self or tongues that fills up the prophecy. Instead of the prophet giving a word that is straight to the point, every other word is full of tongues or their personal opinion. This can be hard to understand at times and leave the recipient of the word confused. Tongues aren't prophecy. This can be clarified in 1 Corinthians 14:2-5. The second don'ts of prophecy is don't speak in excessive tongues. Once I was on a minister's broadcast and she began to prophesy. As she went forth, she started making these loud groaning sounds as she gave words. I was having a difficult time staying focused. The third don'ts of prophecy is don't be too dramatic.

The next don'ts of prophecy is don't lay hands on inappropriate places on the opposite sex. Imagine if you were at the altar receiving prayer and someone of the opposite sex touches your private area. You would immediately become offended and say, "Hold up now or stop it." You could be flowing accurately in the spirit but made a mistake and touched someone the wrong way. They probably won't receive anything you just said. Just be mindful. I have seen men have their wives or another woman lay hands on the women they were ministering too. They just laid their hands on top of theirs to make the women recipient feel comfortable.

The next prophetic don'ts is don't let people worship you. People will be drawn to the gift in you. Your name will spread as the supernatural flows. We must stay humble and always give God the glory. John wanted to worship the angel who brought him the prophetic word. However, the angel warned him to only worship God.

Revelation 22:8-9 says, "And I John saw these things, and heard them. And when I had heard and seen, I fell down to worship before the feet of the angel which shewed me these things. Then saith he unto me, See thou do it not: for I am thy fellowservant, and of thy brethren the prophets, and of them which keep the sayings of this book: worship God."

The same way the angel warned John not to worship anyone but God, we must also follow the same advice. We should never want to hog the mic. One of the protocols of the church is to let two or three prophets speak while the rest judge (1 Corinthians 14:29). You may receive part of the word and God may give another prophet the other piece of the puzzle. We must never release a word contrary to God's word.

2 Peter 1:20-21 says, "Knowing this first, that no prophecy of the scripture is of any private interpretation. For the prophecy came not in old time by the will of man: but holy men of God spake as they were moved by the Holy Ghost."

God confirms things in His word. He would never tell you to sin when His word contradicts that. The next prophetic don'ts is don't mix the word with personal judgment. Once a prophet ministered to me as soon as I got on his periscope. I was receiving everything he said to me in the first few minutes of his prophecy. Then I noticed when he put his flesh into the word. He said, "You can connect with a true prophet as myself because I am the real deal. I don't play around." Another example would be someone who prophesy in error about their personal opinion concerning racism or political matters that contradicts the word of God.

Matthew 7:1-5 says, "Judge not, that ye be not judged. For with what judgment ye judge, ye shall be judged: and with what measure ye mete, it shall be measured to you again. And why beholdest thou the mote that is in thy brother's eye, but considerest not the beam that is in thine own eye? Or how wilt thou say to thy brother, Let me pull out the mote out of thine eye; and, behold, a beam is in thine own eye? Thou hypocrite, first cast out the beam out of thine own eye; and then shalt thou see clearly to cast out the mote out of thy brother's eye."

CHAPTER EIGHT

Prophets and the Other Five-Fold

Prophets need to work together with other five-fold offices. These offices are listed in Ephesians 4:11. We will discuss each of these offices. Whenever the five-fold ministries are discussed, a hand diagram is also referenced. The index, or pointer, finger represents the prophets because this finger often guides just like the prophets in the body of Christ. Many people come to prophets for guidance. Although prophets have a special connection with God, they still need other members in the body of Christ.

The pastor is the next office that we will discuss. The ring finger on the hand diagram represents the pastor. The pastoral office usually clashes the most with the prophetic office. Most pastors are territorial over the people in their congregation and want to protect them. They are very cautious about who speaks into the lives of the people that they are called to oversee. For instance, a shepherd protects the sheep. A pastor has a responsibility and mandate from God to teach, train, and equip the saints in their facilities.

This is the biggest reason that the pastoral and prophetic office clashes because the pastor has to ensure that the prophet has been proven. They have to make sure that the prophet speaks the true word of the Lord. If the pastor allowed anyone who proclaim to be a prophet to release words, then they would be held responsible if that word caused damage and led the people astray. Pastors are more stationary compared to prophets and evangelists. In other words, the pastor is bound to the local saints in a shepherding relationship.

Even though, the prophetic and pastoral offices clash sometimes, they can be complementary when they are yielded to the Holy Spirit. The pastor is the one who usually goes to the weddings, funeral, etc. for the members, but it's usually the prophet who keeps watch and intercedes for the members the most. The pastor has to realize that they don't see everything in the spirit realm and that might lack certain revelation about a particular subject matter. This is why pastors need prophets. A true prophet of God will only want to build up the pastor's vision from the Lord and not take over or cause division in the church.

The next five-fold office is the teacher which represents the little finger. Prophets have to work alongside teachers in the body of Christ. We can see prophets and teachers alongside in the following verse.

Acts 13:1 says, "In the church at Antioch there were prophets and teachers: Barnabas, Simeon called

Niger, Lucius of Cyrene, Manaen (a childhood companion of Herod the tetrarch), and Saul."

It is the teacher who is graced with the ability to make the average person understand the word but it is the prophet who received the revelation and heard what the Lord wanted to teach the people in the congregation.

The evangelist represents the middle finger. The middle finger is the longest finger because it is symbolic of the gathering of souls. It is the evangelist who went and labored in the fields, but it was usually the prophet who intercede for more laborers to bring in the harvest. However, we are all called to do the work of the evangelist (2 Timothy 4:5). We all need to share our faith with someone regardless if we have a title or not.

Mark 16:15 says, "And he said to them, "Go into all the world and proclaim the gospel to the whole creation."

The apostles on the hand diagram is represented by the thumb. The thumb covers all the other fingers. An apostle has a unique ability to flow in the other five-fold offices. Every prophet needs an apostle and every apostle needs a prophet. We can see this relationship between Apostle Paul and Prophet Silas (Acts 16:25-34). Acts 15:32 shows that Silas was a prophet which says, "And Judas and Silas, being prophets also themselves, exhorted the brethren with many words, and confirmed them." God has these two offices working together for divine functions.

Luke 11:49 says, "Therefore also said the wisdom of God, I will send them prophets and apostles, and some of them they shall slay and persecute:"

Ephesians 2:20 says, "And are built upon the foundation of the apostles and prophets, Jesus Christ himself being the chief corner stone;"

In a modern church setting, Apostle would oversee the development and sending of apostolic teams for miracle ministries, as well as activating, imparting and demonstrating the apostolic anointing to other bodies of believers. Apostles function in administration and (together with prophets) lay the foundation with proper doctrinal and spiritual structure. It is the apostle who oversees, or governs, or even builds the blue print that the prophet got out of the realm of the spirit.

CHAPTER NINE

Effective Prophetic Ministry

My biggest prayer is for me to always be effective in ministry. I want lives to be changed for the glory of God. I want God's Glory to manifest each time I preach His word. I want signs and wonders to follow every time I minister the word of God. I have been very fortunate to have all of these things. I never want to grieve the Holy Spirit. Every time I minister God's precious word, I want to always hit the bull's eyes while delivering a powerful pact word that destroys the yoke of the enemy and sets the captive free. I've learned nine ways to have an effective prophetic ministry.

The first thing to be effective is to partner with the Holy Spirit. We have to ensure that He is present. I take the necessary steps to seek God before I minister. I will prepare with my everyday lifestyle of prayer, fasting, and worship just to get in His presence. I never want to make the mistake of moving ahead of God. So many times in life we make major decisions and God is not in them. Then we want to panic and cry out to God for His divine intervention. The Holy Spirit will never lead us astray because He is the spirit of truth.

John 16:13 says, "Howbeit when he, the Spirit of truth, is come, he will guide you into all truth: for he shall not speak of himself; but whatsoever he shall hear, that shall he speak: and he will shew you things to come."

As you read the word of God, the Holy Spirit will begin to highlight things in the bible. Your eyes may open as you receive revelation of new things that you never knew before.

John 14:26 says, "But the Advocate, the Holy Spirit, whom the Father will send in My name, will teach you all things and will remind you of everything I have told you."

Whenever I minister at church, the Holy Spirit will speak to me and give me specific instructions on what He wants me to do in that meeting. I may even receive a vision hours or days beforehand so I know exactly what to do.

1 Corinthians 2:10 says, "But God hath revealed them unto us by his Spirit: for the Spirit searcheth all things, yea, the deep things of God."

As we partner with the Holy Spirit, every person's needs will be met because God's spirit is all knowing.

The second way to have an effective prophetic ministry is to minister in love. 1 Corinthians 12 discusses the spiritual gifts and 1 Corinthians 13 discusses love.

1 Corinthians 13:2 says, "And though I have the gift of prophecy, and understand all mysteries, and all knowledge; and though I have all faith, so that I could remove mountains, and have not charity, I am nothing."

We can be powerful in God but if we don't have love then we are nothing. Remember God is love (1 John 4:8). When you minister in love, people are edified and God is glorified.

Ephesians 4:16 says, "From whom the whole body fitly joined together and compacted by that which every joint supplieth, according to the effectual working in the measure of every part, maketh increase of the body unto the edifying of itself in love."

The third way to have an effective prophetic ministry is not being critical. Whenever we are critical of someone, we make the mistake of being judgmental. The prophecy will not be pure but tainted. The prophecy will be full of the prophesier's fleshy criticism instead of God's heart for the recipient of the prophecy. Just as Jesus was able to not judge by the way things look or what He heard, so can we. Isaiah 11:3 explains this which says, "And shall make him of quick understanding in the fear of the Lord: and he shall not judge after the sight of his eyes, neither reprove after the hearing of his ears." We have to be cautious and seek the Lord's heart on every situation.

Ecclesiastes 5:2 says, "Be not rash with thy mouth, and let not thine heart be hasty to utter any thing before God: for God is in heaven, and thou upon earth: therefore let thy words be few."

Someone could have made a horrible mistake but they repented before God. As a prophet, we are obligated to restore them back to the body of Christ with love and edification. The words of the prophet have an ability to root out, pull down, destroy, and throw down (Jeremiah 1:10). Think before you speak prophet and be careful what you say.

Ephesians 4:29 says, "Let no corrupt communication proceed out of your mouth, but that which is good to the use of edifying, that it may minister grace unto the hearers."

We have to learn how to yield our mouths to God as we are called to be His mouth piece!

The fourth way to have an effective prophetic ministry is to not gossip. There are so many hurting people. They are broken and hopeless. They are searching for answers and will often come to a prophet for counsel. We have to be guards and protects the hearts of God's people. I have witnessed gossip destroy a church. There was a church that I attended years ago that experienced three church splits due to excessive gossip.

People were hurt, including me, because the leaders told all their personal business and misconstrued information about them. Gossiping was the first thing that the Lord dealt with in my life. I remember being a part of a small intercessory team and all we did was gossip about what happened after church service. I was so convicted that I had to quit the team.

Titus 3:2 says, "To speak evil of no man, to be no brawlers, but gentle, shewing all meekness unto all men."

The scriptures warn us not to gossip. Instead of gossiping when someone comes to you with information, just stop them and begin to pray for them. You never want to be caught up in confusion or foolishness.

Proverbs 16:28 says, "A froward man soweth strife: and a whisperer separateth chief friends."

All gossip does is separates friends and causes division.

Proverbs 6:16-19 says, "These six things doth the Lord hate: yea, seven are an abomination unto him: A proud look, a lying tongue, and hands that shed innocent blood, An heart that deviseth wicked imaginations, feet that be swift in running to mischief, A false witness that speaketh lies, and he that soweth discord among brethren."

The Lord hates gossip, so it's best to be pleasing in His sight. Gossiping will cause destruction to any ministry.

The fifth way to have an effective prophetic ministry is to live holy. A holy lifestyle will attract the presence of God. The spoken words from a holy person will yield great produce. You will be surprised that none of your words will hit the ground. A life of holiness produces a life of miracles. Jesus Christ is the epitome of holiness and the miracles He performed were numerous.

Psalm 101:2 says, "I will behave myself wisely in a perfect way. O when wilt thou come unto me? I will walk within my house with a perfect heart."

Prophets have to behave themselves in a perfect (holy) way. Their hearts must stay pure before God.

1 Peter 1:15-16 says, "But as he which hath called you is holy, so be ye holy in all manner of conversation; Because it is written, Be ye holy; for I am holy."

Holiness is a requirement. We must rid ourselves of baggage and allow God to prune us of any sin. We must be dead to sin.

1 Corinthians 3:16-17 says, "Know ye not that ye are the temple of God, and that the Spirit of God dwelleth in you? If any man defile the temple of God, him shall God destroy; for the temple of God is holy, which temple ye are."

Your body is not your own prophet. Your body belongs to God. Be careful of what you watch and hear.

The sixth way to have an effective prophetic ministry is not ministering when you are wounded.

Proverbs 18:14 says, "The spirit of a man will sustain his infirmity; but a wounded spirit who can bear?"

Who wants to be hurt? Whenever I am hurting from rejection, betrayal, or the stressors in life, I take a break. I spend more time than usual in prayer and worship. Even if I am unable to take time off due to speaking engagements or an itinerary that is booked up, I release my pain to God. I refuse to hurt someone else because I am hurting. If I do, then I am accountable to God. There is a saying that hurt people hurt people. That doesn't have to be true in your life. Hurt people should have compassion on other people because they understand how it feels to be hurt. When I was going through a dark time in my life, I encouraged everyone that I could. The Lord blessed me significantly. He never failed to comfort me and to supply all of my needs.

Psalm 147:3 says, "He healeth the broken in heart, and bindeth up their wounds."

God can heal your broken heart and allow you to be effective in the ministry He has for you. God can use your pain to birth your ministry. He can develop purpose out of things you endured.

1 Peter 5:7 says, "Casting all your care upon him; for he careth for you."

Don't hurt people by your pain. Give the burdens to God. I had to preach once when I had been crying for weeks. That was one of the most powerful service where the Glory of God manifested. Many miracles occurred that night. Deaf ears were opened and limbs were straightened. Instead of me causing damage to God's people, the Lord was able to use me in my state of brokenness.

The seventh way to have an effective prophetic ministry is to have a strong and consistent prayer life. How can you be a prophet and not pray? How can you communicate with God if you have no prayer life or a weak prayer life? Prayer is your opportunity to receive from God. Prophets are constantly pouring out but they need God to pour back into them. I love to soak in His presence. I have tons of notebooks full of words that I received from God by spending time in prayer.

1 Thessalonians 5:17 says, "Pray without ceasing."

Even when we are experiencing a resistance in our prayer life, we need to be praying consistently in our heavenly language.

Romans 12:12 says, "Rejoicing in hope; patient in tribulation; continuing instant in prayer;"

Prophets face some of the hardest trials in life. We are called to be intercessors and hopeful. We can't stop praying because of the watchmen assignment that is upon our lives. The basic assignment of a prophet is prayer and intercession.

Ephesians 6:18 says, "Praying always with all prayer and supplication in the Spirit, and watching thereunto with all perseverance and supplication for all saints;"

We need to get our prayer list out and pray.

Colossians 4:2 says, "Continue in prayer, and watch in the same with thanksgiving;"

Our prayers are never in vain. We need to be thankful and remain watchful. The Lord is hearing the prayers of his prophets.

The eighth way to have an effective prophetic ministry is to keep your gifts active.

Proverbs 27:17 says, "Iron sharpeneth iron; so a man sharpeneth the countenance of his friend."

I love to connect with other prophets. My gifts are sharpened as I am around the prophetic anointing. There are three ways to keep your gifts active. Connect to a prophetic ministry; ask and believe God for signs and wonders following; study, attend training, and read books. These three ways have heightened my spiritual gifts. Our gifts need to be exercised. Just as a weight lifter work outs over time, they have built up an increase amount of stamina, muscle mass, and endurance.

The ninth way to have an effective prophetic ministry is to stay abided in God's presence. Whenever I do prophetic events, I prepare early in the morning. I give myself hours before the event to soak up God's presence. When I minister, everyone else that makes contact with me can feel that anointing. Every day, I am blessed to feel the fire of God. If I don't feel Him, then I am seeking Him to feel Him. I prayed to God to never take His fire off my life. God honored that prayer.

Whenever you abide in God's presence, you take His presence wherever you go.

John 14:23 says, "Jesus answered and said unto him, If a man love me, he will keep my words: and my Father will love him, and we will come unto him, and make our abode with him."

We want the Holy Spirit, Jesus, and the Father to come make their abode with us. We want them to come dwell with us.

We need to express our love to God not only with our words but with our actions. Love is an action word.

John 15:4-5 says, "Abide in me, and I in you. As the branch cannot bear fruit of itself, except it abide in the vine; no more can ye, except ye abide in me. I am the vine, ye are the branches: He that abideth in me, and I in him, the same bringeth forth much fruit: for without me ye can do nothing."

We will produce the fruit of an effective ministry when we abide in Him. Lives will be changed.

People will be healed, delivered, and souls will be snatched from hell.

Colossians 2:6 says, "As ye have therefore received Christ Jesus the Lord, so walk ye in him."

It's time to ensure that we take the necessary precautions to walk in Him. Let's walk in the spirit so we don't fulfil the lusts of the flesh (Galatians 5:16).

Unit Two

Different Ways God Speaks

CHAPTER TEN

Prophetic Vehicles

To gain a greater insight of prophecy, we must first gain knowledge of prophetic vehicles. Prophetic vehicles are the ways God brings us his word.[5] God can speak in many different ways. Some people limit God by thinking he only speaks in an audible voice. God has spoken to me through writing, dreams, his fire, and impressions on my body. We will explore these methods and more in this chapter.

To further elaborate, one day a potential courtship opened up for me. At the time, I was not focused on dating but lost in my purpose doing the work of the Lord. A young minister approached me and told me that he was interested. I went to God about it and prayed. Immediately, I heard, "No!" Then I felt a sharp stinging fiery pain go across my arm and it lifted. The sting made me say ouch out loud. Then I knew it was God telling me to not even entertain this young gentleman. A week after that encounter, I found out that this man was married. God warned me and because I listen to his voice and was sensitive to his fiery presence, I was spared from entering a destructive relationship.

There are many synonyms for the word vehicle. Channels, medium, conduit, means, means of expression, agency, agent, instrument, mechanism, organ, or apparatus can be a substitute for this word.[6] When we discuss prophetic vehicles, think of it as different ways God chooses to deliver his word. We don't want to miss God by analyzing everything or being closed minded. We can't allow fear to hinder us from receiving revelation. God moves in different ways.

We can see this in 1 Corinthians 12:4-7 which says, "Now there are diversities of gifts, but the same Spirit. And there are differences of administrations, but the same Lord. And there are diversities of operations, but it is the same God which worketh all in all. But the manifestation of the Spirit is given to every man to profit withal."

There are different spiritual gifts and they all come from God. There are different ministries that have different functions but they still serve the Lord Jesus Christ. There are different ways God speaks, moves through people, or manifests, but everything is working to edify the overall body of Jesus Christ or the church. Now that ,we explained that God moves in different ways, let's look at the different prophetic vehicles that we will discuss in great detail.

Here are some, but not all the ways, God speaks; the voice of God, prophets, dreams, visions, talking unaware, perception, preaching, proxy, writing, parables, prophetic behavior, sealing the word, prayer, angels, the scriptures, and symbolism. When we talk about the voice of God, we can group that into two categories. The internal voice of God which is the still small voice of the Holy Spirit that most people hear in their minds. The other is the external voice of God which is loud and sounds as if someone is beside you talking in the room. The Voice of God is one of the most common ways God speaks to us. As a prophet, I often hear the internal voice. Yet, I have heard the external voice of God about three times in my life.

CHAPTER ELEVEN

External Voice

When I heard God's external voice, it was loud and almost thunderous. My initial response was to be fearful, but I realized that it was God correcting me for my mistakes. Years ago, I wasn't on fire for God like I am now. I had no revelation of what righteousness was or how to live holy. Yet, the hand of the Lord was upon me. I sinned against my own body and tried to hide it from God. God woke me up in the middle of the night and he spoke loudly in my room, "It's not about you!" Since that day, I've made a decision that I will never grieve the Holy Spirit. I realized that my body is the temple of the Holy Ghost and I am not my own. I am thankful that hearing the external voice of God placed his fear in me. Now, I carry a burden of the fear of the Lord. We can find many scriptures discussing the external voice of the Lord.

Psalm 68:33 says, "To Him who rides upon the highest heavens, which are from ancient times; Behold, He speaks forth with His voice, a mighty voice."

The external voice of God is mighty! Think of this voice as a strong thunderous one. When you hear this voice, you might turn around and say, "Who called me?" You might even think someone is in the room with you before you realize that it's God calling you. It's been years since I've heard God's external voice and it was enough to place his holy fear in my heart. Let's look at some scriptures.

Psalm 29:3-9 says, "The voice of the LORD is upon the waters; The God of glory thunders, The LORD is over many waters. The voice of the

LORD is powerful, The voice of the LORD is majestic. The voice of the LORD breaks the cedars; Yes, the LORD breaks in pieces the cedars of Lebanon. He makes Lebanon skip like a calf, And Sirion like a young wild ox. The voice of the LORD hews out flames of fire. The voice of the LORD shakes the wilderness; The LORD shakes the wilderness of Kadesh. The voice of the LORD makes the deer to calve And strips the forests bare; And in His temple everything says, "Glory!"

When the Lord called me to a local body to teach on prophecy and to impart into the members there, I taught on the above scriptures. I had read the psalms multiple times but didn't receive this revelation until it was time for me to train others. I wrote an article for my magazine, "Rejoice Essential Magazine," discussing these scriptures[7].

Now a lot of people are going through trials but the voice of God can be heard through the chaos. This is what it means in verse 3 where it says the Lord is upon the waters. God's voice or a word from God can calm the storm. You could be going through so much, but God's word will give you strength to let you know that He reigns. God will get the glory out of our situations regardless of the schemes of the evil one.

Remember, the Lord's voice is powerful because it's a thunderous mighty voice. When God speaks, all of heaven stands at attention. When God speaks, his counsel will stand. When God speaks, his words don't return to him void. The voice of the Lord is powerful even to break down the most stubborn, impossible, or giant situations. Verse 5 talks about the voice of the Lord breaking down the cedars. Different species of cedar trees will vary on their height and width. We will look at the cedar of Lebanon, Cedrus libani, since it's the species the word often refers to. It can reach 40 m (130 ft) in height and up to 2.5 m (8 ft 2 in) in diameter.[8] That's a giant of a tree, however God's voice can break it down. Remember, this for your personal life.

The Lord's voice can do the impossible. Look at verse 7: the voice of the Lord divides the flames of fire. That seems like an impossible task to me. The great thing is that nothing is impossible with God (Luke 1:37). This is why it's vital to be sensitive to the voice of God. God will speak his plans or purposes about a situation and it's up to us to believe it regardless of what we see in the natural.

Look at verse 8:, the voice of the Lord shakes the wilderness. Imagine, the word of God bringing you out of a dry season. This is what happened to me. For three long years, I was in a wilderness season in Colorado. The Lord spoke to me and told me so many amazing promises such marriage, traveling, and restoration. I am in awe of seeing everything come to fruition.

In verse 9, it says the Lord's voice will cause the hinds to calves. In other words, God's voice has the ability to birth new things. God can speak new ideas that you may not have ever thought of. God has given me new ideas for books, projects, teaching, workshops, marketing, and the list continues. This is power of God's voice. Study Psalm 29 during your devotional time with the Lord, you might hear from God. You may even get the answers you have been seeking for.

One thing that is common with the external voice of God is that it is like thunder. To confirm what we have already mentioned previously, let's look at 2 Samuel 22:14. It says, "The LORD thundered from heaven, And the Most High uttered His voice." When God speaks externally, everyone can hear it or more than one person may hear his voice. This is what happened in Deuteronomy 4:33 which says, "Did ever people hear the voice of God speaking out of the midst of the fire, as thou hast heard, and live?"

When God spoke in this chapter the people were afraid. They didn't want to hear from God themselves but they wanted to hear a prophetic word through the prophet. They felt that they would die if they heard God speak to them out of the fire. Don't allow fear to stop you from seeking God and hearing him speak to you.

Earlier I mentioned that when the voice of God speaks externally, it may sound like someone else is in the room with you. You may answer back and say, "Who is calling me?" We can see this happen in 1 Samuel 3:2-15. When Samuel the prophet was a youth, he heard the external voice of God. He was laying down in the temple near the ark of the covenant. The ark of the covenant was where the presence of the Lord dwelled strongly and it symbolized his presence. That's a key to enhancing your prophetic flow. Stay abided in God's presence just like Samuel did.

The Lord called Samuel three times. The first two times, he ran to Eli the priest. Eli told Samuel that he didn't call his name and for him to go back to bed. However, the third time, Eli realized what was going on. He advised Samuel to say, "Here, I am Lord, your servant is listening." God warned his prophet Samuel about the judgement that was going to take place. You know you are in tuned with God when he tells you his plans. God tells his prophets first before he does anything in the earth (Amos 3:7).

CHAPTER TWELVE

Internal Voice of God

The internal voice of God is the most common way God speaks to us. We know this voice as the voice of the Holy Spirit. I describe this voice as one of the quietest voices in my head. I hear the Holy Spirit in my everyday walk with Him. He warns me of danger. He guides me when I don't have a clue what to do. For instance, when I first started my travel ministry, I was nervous, and I felt like I didn't know what I was doing. However, the Lord felt differently. He knew I was ready for more responsibility. At that time, I had been in ministry for three years and preached faithfully online and at my local church. When doors began to open for me, I leaned into God for his counsel even more.

When I first started traveling, the Holy Spirit told me everything that He wanted to do in those services. He even told me what to do. Once He told me to release the fire of God that was upon my life. He even told me to form a prophecy line where I had the people line up and gave them all a prophetic word one by one. The Holy Spirit even gives me words of knowledge often which I describe in great detail in the "School of The Prophets: A Curriculum for Success."

We can see the Holy Spirit functioning in the following verses that we will be covering in this chapter. The first verse, Acts 13:2 shows how the Holy Spirit gives direction.

Acts 13:2 says, "While they were ministering to the Lord and fasting, the Holy Spirit said, "Set apart for Me Barnabas and Saul for the work to which I have called them."

Barnabas and Saul were two powerful Apostles but in order to be effective and fulfil the calls on their lives, they had to separate to accomplish their next assignment. The Holy Spirit spoke these words through one of the prophets that were present. The next verse that we will discuss is Mark 13:11.

Mark 13:11 says, "When they arrest you and hand you over, do not worry beforehand about what you are to say, but say whatever is given you in that hour; for it is not you who speak, but it is the Holy Spirit."

Jesus warned his disciples that the Holy Spirit will give them words of wisdom that will be exactly the words needed to be spoken in a trial. I can attest of the Holy Spirit giving me words at the right time when needed. Most of the messages that I've preached where given to me the night before and sometimes the day of. His spirit is so spontaneous that I received a lot of words during preaching and it's exactly what someone needed to hear. I couldn't worry about what I was going to say. I just learned to be dependent on Him and allow Him to lead me and flow with Him.

Another example of the voice of the Holy Spirit can be found in Acts 8:29. Philip was a powerful evangelist. Signs and wonders followed him. The Holy Spirit told Philip to go down south to the desert place from Jerusalem to Gaza. As a result of his obedience, an Ethiopian got saved. Philip saw the Ethiopian Eunuch reading the prophecies of the prophet Isaiah. He had lacked an understanding of the prophecy. Philip minister to the Eunuch and even baptized him. Someone's life is depending on your obedience to the Holy Spirit.

Once as I was traveling on an airplane, I had an opportunity to minister to this man who was an ex -Mexican drug cartel or dealer. He told me that, "God allowed me to sit next to you today." I even laid hands on his back and prayed for his healing. The Lord led my steps that day as He did with Philip's. The last few scriptures we will discuss are 1 Kings 19:11-13.

1 Kings 19:11-13 says, "And he said, Go forth, and stand upon the mount before the Lord. And, behold, the Lord passed by, and a great and strong wind rent the mountains, and brake in pieces the rocks before the Lord; but the Lord was not in the wind: and after the wind an earthquake; but the Lord was not in the earthquake: And after the earthquake a fire; but the Lord was not in the fire: and after the fire a still small voice. And it was so, when Elijah heard it, that he wrapped his face in his mantle, and went out, and stood in the entering in of the cave. And, behold, there came a voice unto him, and said, What doest thou here, Elijah?"

When Elijah was discouraged about Jezebel's threat, he heard from the Lord. An angel of the Lord spoke to him and gave him a special meal that strengthen him to fast forty days as he traveled to Mount Sinai which is symbolic of the Mountain of God. The Lord asked Elijah what he was doing there on that Mountain and he passed Elijah several times. However, Elijah realized that the Lord was in a still small voice. This was symbolic of the voice of the Holy Spirit. As we fast as Elijah fasted, our ears are more spiritually inclined to hear what the spirit of the Lord is saying. I must admit that I can hear God very sharply as I fast and pray.

CHAPTER THIRTEEN

Prophets

God often speaks through men or prophets to get his message out. This is called prophecy which is men speaking a divine message as they are led by His spirit.

2 Peter 1:21 says, "For the prophecy came not in old time by the will of man: but holy men of God spake as they were moved by the Holy Ghost."

True prophecy comes from God. This is one of the reasons why prophets are able to prophesy things that are over their head. As I step out in faith and deliver a prophetic word to a total stranger, the prophecy seems to involve a big dream that is simply impossible to achieve without the hand of the Lord. I know that the words spoken out of my mouth didn't originate from me. The amazing thing is that these words are always accurate and true since the Holy Spirit is the spirit of truth (John 16:13).

We can see God speak through many prophets in the Holy Bible. He spoke through Jeremiah, Isaiah, Moses, Aaron, Miriam, Obed, Nathan, David, and the list goes on. Sadly, some people don't believe in prophets and they even feel like none exist. They fail to realize that God is the same God yesterday, today and forevermore (Hebrews 13:8). He doesn't change who He is and He has been using mankind since the beginning of time. God used Mary to give birth to Jesus (Luke 1:26-38). God raised up various judges in His word such as Gideon, Manoah, Deborah, Ehud, Samuel, and many more. Why can't God use men to speak as His oracles or as His prophet?

Let's go through some examples where God spoke a message through His prophets.

Jeremiah 23:28 says, "The prophet that hath a dream, let him tell a dream; and he that hath my word, let him speak my word faithfully. What is the chaff to the wheat? saith the Lord."

God encourages His prophets to speak His word without holding back. He encourages them to be bold and speak His word accurately. Nevertheless, we only need to speak what we see and hear if the Lord permits it. When we do this, we are being good stewards of the word of God. We will discuss dreams and visions later on.

Let's look at two scriptures that establishes God spoke through his prophets, which is still relevant for today. The first scripture is Hebrews 1:1 which says, "God, after He spoke long ago to the fathers in the prophets in many portions and in many ways." The next scripture is Luke 1:70 that says, "As He spoke by the mouth of His holy prophets from of old." God wants to use our mouths to get his message across in the earth. All we have to do is to be an available, obedient, yielded vessel. When the prophet Ezekiel prophesied against the enemy nation Gog, it made reference that the Lord spoke through His servants the prophets.

Ezekiel 38:17 says, "Thus says the Lord GOD, "Are you the one of whom I spoke in former days through My servants the prophets of Israel, who prophesied in those days for many years that I would bring you against them?""

CHAPTER FOURTEEN

Talking Unaware

God doesn't need us to be cognizant to use us. He can use us when we are not aware. Have you ever had a conversation with someone and they reply, "You just brought confirmation to me," "I was just thinking about that this morning," "I had a dream about that." The list goes on and on. God has used me in this way often. It's amazing. All I do is show up and just obey the call on my life. People receive confirmation to the things that are praying for or believing God for. Talking unaware is just confirmation. God just needs a willing vessel. His ways aren't our ways (Isaiah 58:8-9). He knows what we have need of before we come ask of him (Matthew 6:8).

When we talk unaware, we are using our faith in God. This is what the righteous should do which is walking by faith (Roman 1:17). We should be so full of faith to believe God to even use us in dreams. Once I prayed that God would use me in dreams and He answered that prayer. I had several dreams of me ministering, praying, and prophesying to people. I knew that God had used me because these dreams felt so real. People have even come to me testifying that I witnessed to them in a dream. God can use us unaware! Why would God use us this way? Well, He is sovereign. Sometimes His will over ride ours.

CHAPTER FIFTEEN

Reaffirmation

Reaffirmation can be defined as confirmation or ratification of the truth or validity of a prior judgment, decision, etc. It also means the assertion that something exists or is true.[9] God uses witnesses to confirm His word. He often confirms things between two or three witnesses.

2 Corinthians 13:1 says, "This is the third time I am coming to you. In the mouth of two or three witnesses shall every word be established."

Often times as I prophesy something new over someone, some people have a hard time believing it or they haven't even thought about the things that is being prophesied. People always come back to me and say, "Woman of God, someone else just prophesied the same thing you did." This is just God confirming his word. God used two prophets named Judas and Silas to confirm His word to a church in Antioch. Remember, we just discussed how God confirms His word out of the mouth of two or three witnesses.

Acts 15:27 says, "We have sent therefore Judas and Silas, who themselves will also tell you the same things by word of mouth."

The people in the church of Antioch needed encouraged and the words of these two prophets strengthened them.

Acts 15:32 says, "And Judas and Silas, being prophets also themselves, exhorted the brethren with many words, and confirmed them."

Recall what basic prophecy is. It is to edify, exhort, and comfort as seen in 1 Corinthians 14:3.

CHAPTER SIXTEEN

Dreams And Visions

God often speaks to His prophets in dreams and visions. Why? Well let's look at Numbers 12:6. This verse changed my life.

Numbers 12:6 says, "And he said, Hear now my words: If there be a prophet among you, I the LORD *will make myself known unto him in a vision, and will speak unto him in a dream."*

When I first got called as a prophet, I was having all these dreams and visions. Everyone thought I was losing my mind. I was misunderstood. Jesus appeared to me on several occasions. I started having visions about my future and other people that were connected to me. The Holy Spirit led me to Numbers 12:6 and I finally understood why I was having consecutive dreams and visions.

God has been giving His children dreams and visions since the beginning of time. The prophet Joel prophesied it and even Apostle Peter requoted his prophecy on the day of Pentecost.

Joel 2:28 says, "And it shall come to pass afterward, that I will pour out my spirit upon all flesh; and your sons and your daughters shall prophesy, your old men shall dream dreams, your young men shall see visions:"

The spirit of God in someone's life will cause the realm of dreams, visions, and prophecy to come forth in a powerful way. The prophet Isaiah had a heavenly vision when he was called. We can see this in Isaiah 6:1-8. He saw the Lord sitting on a throne. He saw the glory of the Lord with seraphims all around the throne. This is a glorious sight. I was also blessed to have a similar encounter. In my wilderness experience, I was intrigued by the courts of heaven. I studied every teaching I could get my hands on about this subject matter. As I meditated on the word of God, the Lord opened my spiritual eyes. He allowed me to see him sitting on the throne but His face was so bright. It shone bright like the sun. I couldn't look upon his glory.

Abraham was a powerful prophet. God called him His friend three times in scriptures (James 2:23, 2 Chronicles 20:7, Isaiah 41:8). Abraham saw deeply in the spirit and also heard God's voice well. When we look at Genesis 15, we can see how close Abraham and God were. They spent the whole day talking to each other. We can see in verse one how God gave Abraham a vision.

Genesis 15:1 says, "After these things the word of the LORD came to Abram in a vision, saying, "Do not fear, Abram, I am a shield to you; Your reward shall be very great."

Abraham asked God questions in verses 2, 3, and 8. God asked Abraham questions in verses 4, 5,7, 9, 13, 14,15, and 16. Imagine how great you can encounter God if you spent the day with Him. Jacob or Israel, God gave him visions that he will get to see his son Joseph whom he thought was dead.

Genesis 46:2 says, "God spoke to Israel in visions of the night and said, "Jacob, Jacob." And he said, "Here I am."

This is the power of prophetic visions. It has the ability to stir up and bring to life the things which you thought was dead. When I felt like nothing was happening, God gave me visions about my future that gave me strength to hold on. When Moses got called into his assignment, he had a supernatural encounter or vision of the burning bush. The bush did not get physically burned even though it appeared that way in this vision. We can see his experience in the following verses.

Exodus 3:2-3 says, "The angel of the LORD appeared to him in a blazing fire from the midst of a bush; and he looked, and behold, the bush was burning with fire, yet the bush was not consumed. So, Moses said, "I must turn aside now and see this marvelous sight, why the bush is not burned up."

Your visions mean something. Write them down like the Lord told his prophet Habakkuk (Habakkuk 2). Ezekiel was a visionary prophet. He had many supernatural encounters with the Living God and he has seen lots of visions. He was blessed to see the four living creatures (Ezekiel 1:4-14), visions of Jerusalem (Ezekiel 8), a vision of the exiles in Chaldea (Ezekiel 11:24-25), and a vision of the valley of dry bones coming to life (Ezekiel 37:1-10).

Zechariah also had many visions of angels. He had eight-night visions (Zechariah 1:7-6:8). God speaks to some prophets more in dreams. We can see this predominately in the life of Daniel.

Daniel 4:5 says, "I saw a dream and it made me fearful; and these fantasies as I lay on my bed and the visions in my mind kept alarming me."

He was also gifted to interpret dreams. We can see this in Daniel chapter two.

Daniel 2:28 says, "However, there is a God in heaven who reveals mysteries, and He has made known to King Nebuchadnezzar what will take place in the latter days This was your dream and the visions in your mind while on your bed."

He was able to interpret the King's dream when none of the magicians could.

Daniel 2:19 says, "Then the mystery was revealed to Daniel in a night vision. Then Daniel blessed the God of heaven;"

CHAPTER SEVENTEEN

Perception

God often gives a supernatural perception to his children. Perception is the ability to perceive and know. It's amazing how the anointing will cause a download of revelation. You will supernaturally know things about people and how to minister to them effectively. We can see Apostle Paul receiving perception when asked questions about marriage. He supernaturally was imparted the wisdom to answer a question about the non-married or virgins.

1 Corinthians 7:25 says, "Now concerning virgins I have no commandment of the Lord: yet I give my judgment, as one that hath obtained mercy of the Lord to be faithful."

When Gideon was called to be a deliverer of Israel, he had an encounter with an angel and he also heard from God. He prayed for a sign from God to see if God would really use him to deliverer the Israelites from the Midianites. We can see Gideon receiving perception in the following verse.

Judges 6:22 says, "And when Gideon perceived that he was an angel of the LORD, Gideon said, Alas, O Lord GOD! for because I have seen an angel of the LORD face to face."

When God called the young prophet Samuel, God called his name. Samuel didn't recognize the voice of God yet. He thought it was Eli the priest calling him. Eli finally perceived that it was the Lord calling Samuel.

1 Samuel 3:8 says, "And the LORD called Samuel again the third time. And he arose and went to Eli, and said, Here am I; for thou didst call me. And Eli perceived that the LORD had called the child."

Unfortunately, God is speaking often and we aren't in a position to hear his voice.

Job 33:14 says, "For God speaketh once, yea twice, yet man perceiveth it not."

Check your perception! Pray and ask God to bless you to always be sensitive to his presence.

CHAPTER EIGHTEEN

Preaching

God's spirit is so spontaneous. Often times as ministers, He will give us a download of what He would want us to say to His people shortly before the service. This has happened to me several times. I can take notes or write sermons but rarely ever will I use them in a service. The notes are just a safety net that many ministers use to preach. God wants us to rely on His spirit. For instance, you may want to stick to your sermon that you have written down about faith but the Holy Spirit may want to give you words of knowledge because someone needs healing in their body. Or perhaps He wants you to get off topic and preach about deliverance because someone in that service needs to hear that word at that exact moment, but you may want to stick to speaking about faith. Do you see how someone can miss what God wants to do? This is a dangerous place to be. Don't grieve the Holy Spirit.

We have to learn how to preach prophetically. God will give you what to say in the time needed for His people.

Matthew 10:19 says, "But when they deliver you up, take no thought how or what ye shall speak: for it shall be given you in that same hour what ye shall speak."

When we rely on God, He will equip us with what to preach. He will fill our mouths with a divine message. We are commissioned to preach the gospel. We can see this in Mark 16:15 that says, "And He said to them, 'Go into all the world and preach the gospel to all creation'." Jesus told his disciples to go out to preach to the lost.

Matthew 10:5-7 says, "These twelve Jesus sent out after instructing them: Do not go in the way of the Gentiles, and do not enter any city of the Samaritans; but rather go to the lost sheep of the house of Israel. And as you go, preach, saying, 'The kingdom of heaven is at hand.'"

Prophetic evangelism is a powerful thing. God will reveal the secrets things of the heart. Believe that God will give you what you need to minister to His people effectively.

Ephesians 3:7-9 says, "of which I was made a minister, according to the gift of God's grace which was given to me according to the working of His power. To me, the very least of all saints, this grace was given, to preach to the Gentiles the unfathomable riches of Christ, and to bring to light what is the administration of the mystery which for ages has been hidden in God who created all things;"

CHAPTER NINETEEN

Proxy

God can deliver His words in various ways. One way that God deliver's a prophecy word is having someone stand in proxy. A proxy is defined as a person authorized to act for another.[10] In other words, someone one to stand in the gap or another person other than His chosen prophet to speak out the prophecy.

Ezekiel 22:30 says, "And I sought for a man among them, that should make up the hedge, and stand in the gap before me for the land, that I should not destroy it: but I found none."

Why would God need to use a proxy? The prophets of old were often killed or thrown in jail for the words they spoke. God had to make sure that His word got delivered. We can see this happening in the book of Jeremiah. Jeremiah's scribe's name was Baruch. Baruch had to deliver prophecies to King Jekoiakim when Jeremiah wasn't able (Jeremiah 36). God had to use Baruch to speak out the prophecy.

Jeremiah 36:4-6 says, "Then Jeremiah called Baruch the son of Neriah: and Baruch wrote from the mouth of Jeremiah all the words of the LORD, which he had spoken unto him, upon a roll of a book. And Jeremiah commanded Baruch, saying, I am shut up; I cannot go into the house of the LORD: Therefore go thou, and read in the roll, which thou hast written from my mouth, the words of the LORD in the ears of the people in the LORD'S house upon the fasting day: and also thou shalt read them in the ears of all Judah that come out of their cities."

CHAPTER TWENTY

God can deliver His word through writing. There are many times where the Lord will use me to write down prophetic messages. Rejoice Essential Magazine is full of prophetic writing. Writing is just another avenue that God uses to get His word out. Before technology evolved, people relied on writing. They had to wait weeks at a time to communicate. Apostle Paul wrote the epistles, or letters, to the church. A word can be written down and delivered to the recipients just as Baruch did in Jeremiah 36. He wrote down prophecies and delivered them to the wicked King. Now we can use blogs, newsletters, books, magazines, emails, internet, and so on to deliver prophecies. Isaiah wrote down prophecies about the Messiah, Jesus Christ, centuries before He even walked the earth!

Isaiah 9:6-7 says, "For unto us a child is born, unto us a son is given: and the government shall be upon his shoulder: and his name shall be called Wonderful, Counsellor, The mighty God, The everlasting Father, The Prince of Peace. Of the increase of his government and peace there shall be no end, upon the throne of David, and upon his kingdom, to order it, and to establish it with judgment and with justice from henceforth even forever. The zeal of the Lord of hosts will perform this."

Jeremiah's writings reached the nations. God made sure His message came across the right people's hands. Jeremiah's letters reached the captives, priests, prophets, and everyone whom King Nebuchadnezzar had in captivity in Babylon.

Jeremiah 29:1 says, "Now these are the words of the letter that Jeremiah the prophet sent from

Jerusalem unto the residue of the elders which were carried away captives, and to the priests, and to the prophets, and to all the people whom Nebuchadnezzar had carried away captive from Jerusalem to Babylon."

Daniel even read the prophecies of Jeremiah and he was a prophet himself.

Daniel 9:2 says, "In the first year of his reign I Daniel understood by books the number of the years, whereof the word of the LORD came to Jeremiah the prophet, that he would accomplish seventy years in the desolations of Jerusalem."

We are even reading the prophecies of old even in this current age. Apostle Peter read the prophecies of Prophet Joel. We can see this on the day of Pentecost (Acts 2:14-18). We are told in the Book of Revelation that there is a blessing for reading the prophecy.

Revelation 1:3 says, "Blessed is he that readeth, and they that hear the words of this prophecy, and keep those things which are written therein: for the time is at hand."

God spoke in a mysterious way in Daniel chapter 5.

Daniel 5:5 says, "In the same hour came forth fingers of a man's hand, and wrote over against the candlestick upon the plaister of the wall of the king's palace: and the king saw the part of the hand that wrote."

God used His prophet, Daniel, to interpret the writing on the wall which was actual a decree of God's judgment.

Daniel 5:24-26 says, "Then was the part of the hand sent from him; and this writing was written. And this is the writing that was written, Mene, Mene, Tekel, Upharsin. This is the interpretation of the thing: Mene; God hath numbered thy kingdom, and finished it."

We can see Prophet Habakkuk writing down his prophetic vision when he was waiting for the Lord to bring forth justice.

Habakkuk 2:1-3 says, "I will stand upon my watch, and set me upon the tower, and will watch to see what he will say unto me, and what I shall answer when I am reproved. And the Lord answered me, and said, Write the vision, and make it plain upon tables, that he may run that readeth it. For the vision is yet for an appointed time, but at the end it shall speak, and not lie: though it tarry, wait for it; because it will surely come, it will not tarry."

I always encourage people to write down the things they hear in prayer. It could be a word for the nations!

CHAPTER TWENTY ONE

Parables

God's word was often delivered in parables. A parable is a short allegorical story designed to illustrate or teach some truth, religious principle, or moral lesson.[11] It can also be defined as a statement or comment that conveys a meaning indirectly by the use of comparison, analogy, or the like. We can see how parables were the most effective way sometimes to deliver a message. These stories were spiritually discerned. They were so simple but so complexed at the same time. Most carnal people couldn't catch the message within them. Jesus explained this very fact to his disciples.

Matthew 13:10-11 says, "And the disciples came, and said unto him, Why speakest thou unto them in parables? He answered and said unto them, Because it is given unto you to know the mysteries of the kingdom of heaven, but to them it is not given."

In addition, he explains that his parables reveal the mysteries of God just like the prophet Isaiah spoke.

Matthew 13:34-35 says, "All these things spake Jesus unto the multitude in parables; and without a parable spake he not unto them: That it might be fulfilled which was spoken by the prophet, saying, I will open my mouth in parables; I will utter things which have been kept secret from the foundation of the world."

Nathan was a prophet of the Most High God. He was sent to deliver a message to another prophet who was the King. Nathan had to deliver God's message the most effectively way to reach the King who had recently fell into sin with a woman named Bathsheba. He had to make sure his life was not in jeopardy by delivering word of the Lord. Speaking through a parable was the wisest choice. This parable captured David's attention and resulted in his repentance (2 Samuel 12:1-7). Sometimes, telling a story is the best way to draw the hearts and minds of the people before the prophetic word gets released. A parable is a great way to deliver a hard word.

Let's take a detailed look at Matthew 13. Jesus was also a prophet and He used parables. He tells a story about the planting the seed, or ministering the word of God (Matthew 13:1-9). A farmer sowed a seed and four things happened. Some seeds fell by the wayside and birds came and snatched it up. This is symbolic of the message of the gospel that is not even penetrating the hearts and minds of people, and immediately the enemy snatches the word up by distractions or varies cares of this world.

Some seeds fell on stony places. These seeds germinated on top of the rocks but couldn't grow deep and eventually died. Their roots weren't in the soil. How many Christians lack the deep revelatory knowledge of God? How many believers in Christ are still on spiritual milk? When something happens, they walk away from the faith and their whole relationship with God was just superficial. Just like the seed withered and died in the heat so do these Christians die spiritually.

Some seeds fell among the thorns that eventually choked or limited these seeds from fully blossoming. Thorns can be symbolic of cares of this life, distractions, or demonic strongholds. Unfortunately, some believers aren't able to reach their fullest potential in Christ for these very reasons. They want to do right but they always find themselves bound and aren't able to fully mature spiritually.

Lastly, some seeds fell on good ground and produced fruit. Some seed produced more fruit than others. Some produced thirty, sixty, or an hundred times more. The goal of preaching the gospel and allowing the word of God in our hearts is for it to take root. We want to produce the fruits of the spirit. Producing true fruit is becoming more like Christ and less like us.

Jesus explains this parable in Matthew 13:18-23. Jesus warns us in verse 9. He told us to listen. He warns us again in verse 43. We have to listen to what the spirit of the Lord is saying through His parables. We have to be in tuned with His spirit. Let's look at Matthew 13:13-17. Jesus further explains why He teaches in parables. People can miss God right in front of their eyes! That's a scary place to be. In other words, He said, "They see but are not seeing. They hear and aren't hearing. They aren't comprehending the meaning of my messages but I have blessed my disciples to understand them." We can't allow our hearts to be hardened or our hearing to be dull towards God's word. Before we even begin reading our bible, we should ask God for revelation of the scriptures so we can grow and produce fruit in our lives.

Jesus tells another parable about the wheat and the tares (Matthew 13:24-30). Who would've thought that this story would be like how the kingdom of heaven operates? There will eventually be a separation from the good (wheat) and the bad (tares). The enemy may plant tares among the wheat as they are going through their growing stage, however a time will come will the tares will meet their fate. They will be burned up and only the wheat will make it into the barn. This is how it is in this world. We may be in an evil world, but one day we will make it to heaven if we live right, receive salvation, and obey God. Jesus further explains this parable in verses 37 to 43. We also see more separating the good from the bad in Matthew 13:47-50 in the parable of the fishing net.

Jesus tells a parable about the mustard seed in verses 31-32. The smallest seed can grow into a big tree where birds will come make their home in. This is symbolic to God using what seems to be the least important and making it into something great. When I felt insecure, ashamed, and broken from the trials, I endured in life, God gave me another chance and placed greatness within me. God can use you to do a great work for Him no matter how insignificant you feel your background may be!

Another parable we should look at is in verse 33. It is the parable of the yeast. It is short and simple. However, it is complex because it is spiritually discerned. A woman tried to hide the yeast among the flour but eventually it all rose. The yeast in the flour eventually got exposed. No matter how much we try to hid sin in our lives, we can't hide it from God! If we aren't careful to allow God to deal with these matters it will ruin us in the long run. As a prophet, we have to give God our insecurities, fear, pain, and the list goes on. We don't want to be corrupt or tainted. Lives are at stake! Those sins will eventually be exposed if we try to hide it and continue to do things that aren't pleasing to God.

In verse 44, a person finds some treasure in a field and sells everything to make sure they have enough to buy that field. This is how it is like for a prophet to go through training and testing. We have to be willing to give everything up to fulfil our call. We can find joy when we embrace God's plan for our lives. I often tell the Lord that I am willing to pay the price! I have lost everything to follow after Christ and I have joy knowing that I am walking in my purpose despite the adversity. In verses 45-46, a merchant finds a valuable pearl. He sold everything he had to buy it. Jesus's disciples walked away from everything to follow him. It may seem like we are losing but we are actually gaining (Philippians 3:8).

CHAPTER TWENTY TWO
Prophetic Action

Sometimes God has His prophets do certain things to illustrate His word. The life of the prophet can become a prophetic action. They can even express prophetic action through certain behaviors. Prophetic action can be defined as a prophet illustrating the prophetic message. God can use his prophet to become a visual aid. Action can be defined as the accomplishment of a thing usually over a period of time, in stages, or with the possibility of repetition.[11] Prophetic actions can have different durations of time. For instance, the Prophet Agabus bound up his own hands and feet using Apostle's Paul belt as a way to tell him that if he would go to Jerusalem, he would be bonded in chains or jailed. Apostle Paul didn't heed to the prophetic word or the cries of the people who witnessed this prophecy. He was extremely zealous and wanted the will of God to be done in his life (Acts 21:10-14).

Let's take a look at the book of Hosea. The marriage of Hosea and Gomer appeared to last over a long time. His whole marriage was a symbolic act or prophetic action. He and Gomer had three children with prophetic names. His marriage to Gomer was a prophetic indication of Israel's adulterous state. They were worshipping pagan gods and forgot about the covenant their ancestors had with God. God told the prophet Hosea to marry a prostitute and then he told him to go get his wife back! This is God's love is for his people. He stills loves us even when we turn our backs on him. God sometimes will pursue us relentlessly just like he did with the Israelites because his love for us runs so deep. Would you be willing to allow your life, marriage, and children to be used as a prophetic action if God commanded you to do so? This is a very difficult decision to make.

Let's look at Ezekiel Chapter 4. Ezekiel the prophet had to lay on his side tied up with ropes for many days as a warning of the exile to Babylon. He had to lay on his left side for three hundred and ninety days to symbolize the sins of the house of Israel. Also, he had to lay on his right side for forty days to symbolize the siege of Jerusalem. He had to ration his drink and water as he lied on his side. This was symbolic of the famine that would come and the people had to eat and drink the food and water that was measured out to them. Ezekiel also had to bake bread using cow's feces for the fire and eat it to symbolize the unclean food that the children of Israel will have to eat. Remember, God's ways aren't our ways. We may not understand something initially, but as we walk with God, we will come more into an understanding.

Would you be willing to cut all your hair off and throw it around the city? This is what happened in Ezekiel 5. He had to shave all his hair off his head and beard, divide it into three parts and weigh it. When he was instructed to throw his hair into the winds, it was symbolic of how God would chase the Israelites with his sword. When Ezekiel burned some of his hair in the fire, it was a prophetic act of how God would cause a fire to spread through Jerusalem.

The prophet Isaiah had to do something that most of us would be uncomfortable to do. He had to walk around naked for three years as a sign that Assyria would take Egypt and Cush into captivity. The people would be ashamed and naked. Another example of prophetic action can be seen in the book of Jeremiah. Jeremiah bought a piece of land to bring home a prophetic message (Jeremiah 32:1-9). We see an example of a prophet who was commanded by God to tell people to hit him. Once he got hit, he could then disguise himself to deliver a hard word to King Ahab (1 Kings 20:35-42). Prophets will appear to behave oddly to some, remember, God has a plan.

CHAPTER TWENTY THREE

Sealing the Word

Every revelation that we receive in prayer is not meant to be shared. Sometimes we have to hold on to a word for a while before the Holy Spirit allows us to release it. We should not assume that because we have been given a word that we have permission to share it. We must ask the Holy Spirit what He wants us to do with the prophetic word. Oftentimes, the prophecy is sealed up for another time. This is called sealing the word. Sometimes a word must be sealed up for delivery at a later time. The prophet Daniel was told to seal up some of his words for the future.

Daniel 12:9 says, "He replied, 'Go your way, Daniel, because the words are closed up and sealed until the time of the end.'"

It's acceptable to write down the prophetic word for a later date. Sometimes, the prophetic word will manifest at a later date.

Habakkuk 2:3-4 says, "For the vision is yet for an appointed time, but at the end it shall speak, and not lie: though it tarry, wait for it; because it will surely come, it will not tarry. Behold, his soul which is lifted up is not upright in him: but the just shall live by his faith."

On many occasions, I wrote down the prophecies and they manifested a great while later.

CHAPTER TWENTY FOUR

Prayer

God speaks to us through prayer. Many times, we can receive the answer we are seeking by spending time in prayer. Often times as I pray, the prophetic word just comes out and I begin to prophesy. Prophets must have a strong prayer life. It is mandatory. Daniel had a strong prayer life. He was able to get solutions to the problems that he encountered. This prophet served in the King's court and God used him to deliver messages to various Kings. These messages often came through prayer. Let's look at the following verses.

Daniel 2:16-18 says, "Then Daniel went in, and desired of the king that he would give him time, and that he would shew the king the interpretation. Then Daniel went to his house, and made the thing known to Hananiah, Mishael, and Azariah, his companions: That they would desire mercies of the God of heaven concerning this secret; that Daniel and his fellows should not perish with the rest of the wise men of Babylon."

The King had a disturbing dream and wouldn't tell anyone his dream. He called for the astrologers, diviners, magicians, the wise men, and wizards. He threatened them with death unless they could tell him the dream and the meaning. Daniel knew that God could interpret the dream but it would take time in prayer. God gave Daniel the answer in a dream later that night after he sought Him in prayer (Daniel 2:19). God blessed Daniel with a tremendous promotion. His territory was enlarged.

Daniel 2:48 says, "Then the king made Daniel a great man, and gave him many great gifts, and made him ruler over the whole province of Babylon, and chief of the governors over all the wise men of Babylon."

As you spend time in prayer, step out in faith and get a notebook. Expect God to speak to you and be prepared to write down what you hear in prayer.

CHAPTER TWENTY FIVE

Angels

God has special messengers called angels.

Psalm 103:20 says, "Bless the Lord, ye his angels, that excel in strength, that do his commandments, hearkening unto the voice of his word."

Angels are ready to serve God and obey His every command. To keep it simple, we are just discussing good angels, not evil fallen angels. Angels are ministering spirits and they are here to help believers.

Hebrews 1:14 says, "Are they not all ministering spirits, sent forth to minister for them who shall be heirs of salvation?"

Many of us might be aware of their presence or when they enter into a room without seeing them with our physical eyes. We might be blessed to see their form with our spiritual eyes. I often see angels in the spirit realm as I go forth and minister deliverance. One day, I am looking forward to having an angelic encounter just like the following scriptures that we are about to exam. God used angels to deliver His word or His plans for people's lives.

Let's look at Luke 1:26-38. The virgin Mary had an angelic encounter with the archangel Gabriel. This angel told her that she was highly favored, the Lord was with her, she was blessed, she would bring forth a son, and to name him Jesus. When she saw this angel, she was afraid, which is the normal reaction of people who have had angelic encounters throughout scripture. The angel told her who Jesus was and how she would conceive. The angel even told her about her cousin Elizabeth being pregnant. God choose an angel to deliver a prophetic message concerning His plans for the lives of Mary and Elizabeth. It is highly possible for him to do the same with us.

The next example of God using angels to deliver His word is in Luke 1:11-19. Zacharias was a priest and serving in the temple when he had an angelic encounter. He immediately became afraid when he saw the angel, but the angel reassured him that he didn't have to be afraid. This angel, named Gabriel, told Zacharias that his wife Elizabeth who was old in age would conceive a son. Gabriel caused Zacharias to be mute until the baby was born since he didn't believe him. The power of a prophetic word is God's ability to see way beyond than we are able. God's plan for our lives are way better than our own.

Usually when we receive a true prophetic word, we aren't able to comprehend it initially. The word usually goes beyond our natural understanding. We might even think among ourselves, "How can this possibly be?" "This just doesn't make sense?" This is what Zacharias did, and the angel muted him until the prophetic message manifested. Don't allow your words to abort your prophetic promises.

God will send angels when His children are in distress. In Genesis 16, God sent an angel to deliver a word to Hagar who was Sarai's maid. She had run away because she was being mistreated. This angel delivered a prophetic promise over her son Ishmael. God is concerned with the outcast or the people who weren't chosen initially for the promise. Since God is so merciful, He is able to bless the rejects or the people in society that have been overlooked. Even though Isaac had the birth right, God still had a plan for Ishmael. God can still bless us exceedingly even though we might not have been originally chosen. In other words, someone else decided not to walk in what God had for them and God gave it to you. God is looking for people to say yes to the call. Just as Ishmael was the less likely person for God to multiply his seed, God can do something great in our lives.

The prophet Zechariah had many angelic visitations (Zechariah 1:7-6:15). These angels would deliver the meaning, or the interpretation, of the visions that he was seeing. When you study the book of Zechariah, there is a pattern. He would have a vision and ask the Lord, "What are these?" or "What does this mean?" Then the angel would always give him the meaning. For instance, in Zechariah 1:7-17, this prophet had a vision of horses. The angel gave him the interpretation. The angel of the Lord further engages in a conversation with the Lord and instructs the prophet what to prophesy. Zechariah had a strong grace for angels because most people aren't able to handle those types of encounters. Almost everyone in scripture that had an angelic visitation became afraid at first, but the angel encouraged them not to be afraid. We just saw this in Luke 1 when Gabriel visited Mary and Zacharias.

CHAPTER TWENTY SIX

The Scriptures

God delivers His messages throughout the bible. How many times have you opened your bible and was supernaturally led somewhere to get an understanding or revelation about something you just witnessed or the answer to your problem. This has happened to me on many occasions. God will supernaturally highlight a scripture to me as I read the bible or I gained revelation about something. Once in a dream, God spoke to me and told me to read Psalms 106:11.

Psalm 106:11 says, "And the waters covered their enemies: there was not one of them left."

Receiving this scripture was critical for me. I had just launched a new television show called, "Warfare Strategies." I was seeking God on weapons in the bible. I received revelation that God used water as a weapon in his word. I had received the answer that I was looking for. I did research and was able to do a successful broadcast.

God's word is alive, and he has all the answers we need.

Hebrews 4:12 says, "For the word of God is quick, and powerful, and sharper than any two-edged sword, piercing even to the dividing asunder of soul and spirit, and of the joints and marrow, and is a discerner of the thoughts and intents of the heart."

God knows how to speak to us at the right moment. His word carries His thoughts and His heart. As we take time to meditate on scripture daily after we read, the word of God begins to take root in our hearts.

2 Timothy 3:16-17 says, "All scripture is given by inspiration of God, and is profitable for doctrine, for reproof, for correction, for instruction in righteousness: That the man of God may be perfect, thoroughly furnished unto all good works."

The scriptures will equip us to do the work of the gospel if we receive a revelation of what these verses are saying. God will give you the right message for you to deliver at the right moment. The whole bible is prophetic in whole. The prophets in the Old Testament (Book of Genesis to the Book of Malachi) confirm the coming of a Messiah through prophecy. Their prophecy originated from God and not themselves.

2 Peter 1:20- 21 says, "Knowing this first, that no prophecy of the scripture is of any private interpretation. For the prophecy came not in old time by the will of man: but holy men of God spake as they were moved by the Holy Ghost."

As we read the word, we can amazingly see how the prophecy of the Messiah came into fruition. God's plan will always prevail. God's word is a light and provides guidance.

Psalm 119:105 says, "Thy word is a lamp unto my feet, and a light unto my path."

This is how the prophetic works. You may be in a dark season and the prophetic word is giving you a ray of hope. You may have to make a major decision yet the prophetic word will provide guidance. Perhaps you may have read a biblical story and gained strength and courage for your circumstances. Reading the word of God strengthens our trust in God. His word is pure and will shield us from demonic attacks.

Proverbs 30:5- 6 says, "Every word of God is pure: he is a shield unto them that put their trust in him. Add thou not unto his words, lest he reprove thee, and thou be found a liar."

Unit Three

True Characteristic Of A Prophet

CHAPTER TWENTY SEVEN

Characteristics of A True Prophet of God

Over the next several chapters, we will discuss characteristics of a true prophet of God. Many people aren't able to discern the real from the fake. People are caught up in popularity and the gifting of an individual. Characteristics can be defined as a distinguishing trait, quality, or property.[13] Some synonyms of the word characteristics include attribute, feature, quality, essential quality, property, and trait.[14] In other words, characteristics are things across the board that a prophet must have.

The best way to discern a true prophet of God from a false prophet is to look at the fruit. The fruit of the spirit is discussed in Galatians 5:22-25 says, "But the fruit of the Spirit is love, joy, peace, longsuffering, gentleness, goodness, faith, meekness, temperance: against such there is no law. And they that are Christ's have crucified the flesh with the affections and lusts. If we live in the Spirit, let us also walk in the Spirit."

A prophet of God has these attributes in their lives. We will cover each fruit of the spirit and how they can be incorporated into the prophetic in great detail in the upcoming chapters. We must be a fruit inspector. We have to examine whether or not the prophet has evidence of the fruit of the spirit. Don't get caught up in gifts or titles. The devil can prophesy.

Revelation 2:20 says, "Notwithstanding I have a few things against thee, because thou sufferest that woman Jezebel, which calleth herself a prophetess, to teach and to seduce my servants to commit fornication, and to eat things sacrificed unto idols."

Jezebel called herself a prophetess but she wasn't a prophet of God. She had her own prophets. This is why she hated Prophet Elijah so much because he killed the four hundred and fifty prophets of Baal and four hundred prophets of Asherah (1 Kings 18:19).

Elijah killed the prophets that ate at her table. False prophets can prophesy accurately. Beware of those prophets that will prophesy to you and then try to seduce you. That's why character triumphs over gifting. In Matthew 7, we are warned about false prophets.

Matthew 7:16 says, "Ye shall know them by their fruits. Do men gather grapes of thorns, or figs of thistles?"

Grapes don't come from thorn bushes. Figs don't come from weeds. Good and evil don't mix. Light and dark don't mix. Either you are a prophet of the true living God or not. Gifting has nothing to do with character.

Romans 11:29 says, "For the gifts and calling of God are without repentance."

A prophet can start off on the right track and deviate along the way. They may be able to prophesy very accurately but be full of the devil. Balaam is the best example of a prophet who lacked the characteristics that we mentioned earlier. He started off right but allowed greed to overtake him (Jude 11). He eventually led God's children astray.

Numbers 31:16 says, "Behold, these caused the children of Israel, through the counsel of Balaam, to commit trespass (sexual immorality and idolatry) against the Lord in the matter of Peor, and there was a plague among the congregation of the Lord."

A true prophet of God would never promote sexual immorality, idolatry, and other sins. Instead they will encourage people to follow the word of God. In addition to covering the fruit of the spirit in great detail, we will discuss brokenness, humility, servants, faith filled, courageous, wise, spirit lead, obedient to God, integrity, compassion, commitment, righteousness, and surrendered.

CHAPTER TWENTY EIGHT
Love

We have already stated that ministering in love is one way to have an effective prophetic ministry. When we minister in love people are more eager to receive the prophetic word. Attitude makes all the difference on how a prophetic word is received sometimes. I don't want anyone prophesying to me with a nasty attitude. Apostle Paul encouraged us to desire spiritual gifts but he also pushed us to operate in love because it's the best way. It's God's way.

1 Corinthians 12:31 says, "But covet earnestly the best gifts: and yet shew I unto you a more excellent way."

Apostle Paul told us to follow after love.

1 Corinthians 14:1 says, "Follow after charity, and desire spiritual gifts, but rather that ye may prophesy."

He even said that love is the greatest compared to faith and hope.

1 Corinthians 13:13 says, "And now abideth faith, hope, charity, these three; but the greatest of these is charity."

When we minister in love, we represent Christ. Jesus always ministered in love and He had great results. We must be Christ centered and care about the things that He cares about.

Ephesians 3:17 says, "That Christ may dwell in your hearts by faith; that ye, being rooted and grounded in love."

Love must be the motivation behind why we prophesy; not money or fame. We prophesy for God's Glory. When we walk in love, we imitate Christ. It produces a sweet smelling sacrifice up to the throne room of God.

Ephesians 5:2 says, "And walk in love, as Christ also hath loved us, and hath given himself for us an offering and a sacrifice to God for a sweet smelling savour."

Think of all the times when you could've operated in your flesh when someone was nasty towards you. If you decided to not act out but expressed God's love, then you past the love test. You presented yourself a living sacrifice. You allowed God to reign in you and allowed your flesh to die. Jesus prayed for his crucifiers on the cross (Luke 23:34). Are you able to pray for your enemies? Are you able to show your haters the love of God? Are you able to show God's love to the people who are ridiculing, rejecting, or betraying you? Ask God to help you in this area. Love is the most powerful manifestation of God.

John 2:9-11 says, "He that saith he is in the light, and hateth his brother, is in darkness even until now. He that loveth his brother abideth in the light, and there is none occasion of stumbling in him. But he that hateth his brother is in darkness, and walketh in darkness, and knoweth not whither he goeth, because that darkness hath blinded his eyes."

Don't be deceived. You can't say you love God and hate people. To reiterate, love is an action word. If you are wounded and hurt, ask God to put His love in your heart for the person that hurt you. You will be able to forgive them. You will even find yourself praying for them. Let it go. Hating is not an option as a true prophet of God. Prophets love the sinner but hate the sin. The same way God does.

1 John 3:14-17 says, "We know that we have passed from death unto life, because we love the brethren. He that loveth not his brother abideth in death. Whosoever hateth his brother is a murderer: and ye know that no murderer hath eternal life abiding in him. Hereby perceive we the love of God, because he laid down his life for us: and we ought to lay down our lives for the brethren. But whoso hath this world's good, and seeth his brother have need, and shutteth up his bowels of compassion from him, how dwelleth the love of God in him?"

Prophets, just as Jesus came and gave of himself, we too should be willing. Multiple needs were fulfilled when people encountered him. We need to share the love of God with our gifts the Lord has giving us. If you don't have the resources to bless the poor, at least pray for the sick and those who have needs. A true prophet of God would never shut up his bowels of compassion on people. They will never overlook someone who needs help. When you have the ability to be a blessing to someone, then you should. God will be pleased. It was the love of God that operated through my former pastor. Many lives were impacted through him and won to the Lord. Imagine how powerful the prophetic anointing will be in your life if you make it about love!

CHAPTER TWENTY NINE

Prophets need to express traits of joy regardless of their situations. They need the joy of the Lord. Many people will cross paths with the Lord's prophets. Yet, the prophet is called to have delight in God and His word. It's in Christ that we find joy.

Proverbs 10:28 says, "The hope of the righteous shall be gladness: but the expectation of the wicked shall perish."

I have been at rock bottom but still had the joy of the Lord. I didn't know where my next meal would come from. I was sleeping on the floor for years because I didn't have enough money at the time to get a bed. I was thousands of miles away from my family. However, I had the joy of the Lord. I was able to encourage someone else even though I was going through my own set of trials.

1 Peter 1:8 says, " Whom having not seen, ye love; in whom, though now ye see him not, yet believing, ye rejoice with joy unspeakable and full of glory:"

When I think about Jesus, I get the strength to continue in my call as a prophet despite the opposition.

Nehemiah 8:10 says, "Then he said unto them, Go your way, eat the fat, and drink the sweet, and send portions unto them for whom nothing is prepared: for this day is holy unto our Lord: neither be ye sorry; for the joy of the Lord is your strength."

Prophets are able to rejoice at the promises of God because they have already seen what God is doing. No matter what adversity we face, we must be able to lean on God to receive joy. We have to look through eyes of faith. God will fill you with joy, prophet.

Romans 15:13 says, "Now the God of hope fill you with all joy and peace in believing, that ye may abound in hope, through the power of the Holy Ghost."

People are looking at our lives. They are examining if we really believe what we preach. It's a blessing to be able to have joy during the dark times. David found joy in the Lord in Psalm 98. He had to encourage himself in the Lord. This is what we have to do as well. We have to constantly bring the Lord's promises before our eyes and thank Him in advance for our promises. The Lord loves us so much, and He delights to give us joy (Zephaniah 3:14-20).

CHAPTER THIRTY

Peace

A prophet is called to have peace and not worry.

Philippians 4:6-7 says, "Be careful for nothing; but in every thing by prayer and supplication with thanksgiving let your requests be made known unto God. And the peace of God, which passeth all understanding, shall keep your hearts and minds through Christ Jesus."

Why worry when you know that God will take care of things? This is my mind set. There were times when my gas tank was almost on empty. I had no money, but I still got in the car and went to my destination. While I was on the way to my destination, God always sent the money. He made sure that I would make it back home and that I wouldn't be stranded. The most important thing is that I had peace. I wasn't worried about where the money would come from. I just said, "God, thank you for blessing me with gas."

Psalm 29:11 says, "The LORD will give strength unto his people; the LORD will bless his people with peace."

Prophets are able to trust God and the more we get to know Him, the more confident we are in Him.

2 Corinthians 4:8 says, "We are troubled on every side, yet not distressed; we are perplexed, but not in despair;"

Yes, we go through trials. Yes, we have to suffer. But, these things should never steal our peace.

Psalm 4:8 says, "I will both lay me down in peace, and sleep: for thou, LORD, only makest me dwell in safety."

God gives so much peace that we are able to sleep well at night. We could be in a dry season but the Lord will give us strength and give us stability.

Habakkuk 3:17-19 says, "Although the fig tree shall not blossom, neither shall fruit be in the vines; the labour of the olive shall fail, and the fields shall yield no meat; the flock shall be cut off from the fold, and there shall be no herd in the stalls: Yet I will rejoice in the Lord, I will joy in the God of my salvation. The Lord God is my strength, and he will make my feet like hinds' feet, and he will make me to walk upon mine high places. To the chief singer on my stringed instruments."

CHAPTER THIRTY ONE

Longsuffering

Prophets need to be patient. We have to be patient to hear from God at times. The prophet Habakkuk was patient as he waited on what God would show him (Habakkuk 2:1-4). Daniel had to wait to 21 days for an answer to his prayer.

Daniel 10:12-13 says, "Then said he unto me, Fear not, Daniel: for from the first day that thou didst set thine heart to understand, and to chasten thyself before thy God, thy words were heard, and I am come for thy words. But the prince of the kingdom of Persia withstood me one and twenty days: but, lo, Michael, one of the chief princes, came to help me; and I remained there with the kings of Persia."

We need to be patient to wait for the fruition of the prophetic word. Prophets have to be able to accept or tolerate delays, problems, or suffering without becoming annoyed or anxious.

James 5:10-11 says, "Take, my brethren, the prophets, who have spoken in the name of the Lord, for an example of suffering affliction, and of patience. Behold, we count them happy which endure. Ye have heard of the patience of Job, and have seen the end of the Lord; that the Lord is very pitiful, and of tender mercy."

Sometimes, we have to suffer as we wait on the promises. This is part of producing fruit of the Holy Spirit.

Colossians 3:12 says, "Put on therefore, as the elect of God, holy and beloved, bowels of mercies, kindness, humbleness of mind, meekness, longsuffering;"

God may have given you a promise, but it may take years before it happens. This is what happened with Abraham. He waited years for His prophecy to come to pass.

Hebrews 6:15 says, "And so, after he had patiently endured, he obtained the promise."

It may look as if the promise will never come to pass, but we have to stay in faith. We have to believe it before we see it.

Romans 8:25 says, "But if we hope for that we see not, then do we with patience wait for it."

God has a plan and sometimes He has us planted where He wants us. We just have to trust His plan.

Romans 12:12 says, "Rejoicing in hope; patient in tribulation; continuing instant in prayer;"

When we are worrying, we aren't resting in God. God wants to give our souls rest.

Psalm 37:7 says, "Rest in the Lord, and wait patiently for him: fret not thyself because of him who prospereth in his way, because of the man who bringeth wicked devices to pass."

CHAPTER THIRTY TWO

Gentleness

Prophets need to express gentleness. This is the quality of being kind, tender, or mild-mannered.[15] Jesus expressed kindness. He wasn't rude or arrogant. He wasn't pushy or controlling. Why do we struggle in this area? Why do we feel like we have to cut people off to get our point across? Why do we have to over talk people or feel like we have to get the last word in? God will have us to be silent many times when we are being ridiculed or in a disagreement. God wants to fight for us (Exodus 14:14). We can be bold but meek at the same time. Apostle Paul states that in 2 Corinthians 10:1 which says, "Now I Paul myself beseech you by the meekness and gentleness of Christ, who in presence am base among you, but being absent am bold toward you:"

I am an introvert and don't want the spot light. However, when the anointing comes upon me, all of that goes out the window. I begin to walk in a boldness while being gentle.

2 Timothy 2:24-26 says, "And the servant of the Lord must not strive; but be gentle unto all men, apt to teach, patient, In meekness instructing those that oppose themselves; if God peradventure will give them repentance to the acknowledging of the truth; And that they may recover themselves out of the snare of the devil, who are taken captive by him at his will."

Prophets don't have time to get caught up in foolishness. There is no time for distractions. We have the Lord's work to do. Sometimes, prophets feel like they need to pull a rank card. You don't have to try to control people to prove how powerful you are. It's not about you but about Christ. The Apostles in the Thessalonian Church didn't pull a rank card or throw their weight in the spirit around instead they used gentleness to express their message.

1 Thessalonians 2:6-8 says, "Nor of men sought we glory, neither of you, nor yet of others, when we might have been burdensome, as the apostles of Christ. But we were gentle among you, even as a nurse cherisheth her children: So being affectionately desirous of you, we were willing to have imparted unto you, not the gospel of God only, but also our own souls, because ye were dear unto us."

CHAPTER THIRTY THREE

Goodness

Prophets have to produce the fruit of goodness in their lives.

Ephesians 5:8-10 says, "For ye were sometimes darkness, but now are ye light in the Lord: walk as children of light: (For the fruit of the Spirit is in all goodness and righteousness and truth;) Proving what is acceptable unto the Lord."

Goodness is defined as moral excellence; virtue, kindly feeling; kindness; generosity, excellence of quality, doing good to others.[16] We need to share the gifts that God has placed inside of us. We have to be aware that our gifts are not for sale but for the Glory of God. We need to do great works and great exploits for the Lord.

Psalm 33:4-5 says, "For the word of the Lord is right; and all his works are done in truth. He loveth righteousness and judgment: the earth is full of the goodness of the Lord."

We need to share the goodness of the Lord with others. How can we share the goodness of the Lord? Just be available for God to use you. Elisha allowed God to use him. He caused a dead child to live (2 Kings 4:8-37). He made poisonous food safe (2 Kings 4:38-41). By God's power, Elisha cured Naaman who was the captain of a foreign army (2 Kings 5). Never feel like you can't operate in your call if you aren't paid. As you do the right thing, God is pleased.

CHAPTER THIRTY FOUR

Faithful

Prophets have to be found faithful. The call of a prophet requires faithfulness.

1 Corinthians 4:1-2 says, "Let a man so account of us, as of the ministers of Christ, and stewards of the mysteries of God. Moreover it is required in stewards, that a man be found faithful."

Prophets go through a lot trials and tribulations. Prophets need to stay faithful to their assignment despite the opposition. Jesus warns us that we will go through things but to remain faithful unto death.

Revelation 2:10 says, "Fear none of those things which thou shalt suffer: behold, the devil shall cast some of you into prison, that ye may be tried; and ye shall have tribulation ten days: be thou faithful unto death, and I will give thee a crown of life."

The prophet Hosea was faithful when God told him to marry a whore.

Hosea 1:2 says, "The beginning of the word of the Lord by Hosea. And the Lord said to Hosea, Go, take unto thee a wife of whoredoms and children of whoredoms: for the land hath committed great whoredom, departing from the Lord."

Most people wouldn't want to have their marriage symbolize God's relationship with Israel. It took a level of faithfulness to obey God when something is out of our comfort zones. The prophet Jeremiah had to give up fleshly desires for the call of God on his life. He wasn't allowed to have a wife or children. How many people could sacrifice of themselves in this manner and remain faithful to the assignment?

Jeremiah 16:2 says, "Thou shalt not take thee a wife, neither shalt thou have sons or daughters in this place."

Proverbs 28:20 says, "A faithful man shall abound with blessings: but he that maketh haste to be rich shall not be innocent."

Your faithfulness to God will pay off. There is a reason for the trials. There is a lesson in them. When I wanted to give up, the Holy Spirit gave me comfort. He ensured that He was with me. He equipped me for every task. He gave me strength and the anointing to accomplish the task before me. If God did it for me, then why can't He do it for you?

Psalm 37:28 says, "For the Lord loveth judgment, and forsaketh not his saints; they are preserved for ever: but the seed of the wicked shall be cut off."

The Lord will never forsake His people.

CHAPTER THIRTY FIVE

Meekness

Meekness is a great characteristic to have. The word of God tells us to follow after it.

1 Timothy 6:11 says, "But thou, O man of God, flee these things; and follow after righteousness, godliness, faith, love, patience, meekness."

What exactly is meekness? It can be defined as humbly patient, tame, overly submissive or compliant.[17] Jesus, who is the ultimate example of our faith, was meek.

Matthew 11:29 says, "Take my yoke upon you, and learn of me; for I am meek and lowly in heart: and ye shall find rest unto your souls."

A person who is meek will not mind submitting to those who God has placed over them. They know that God is a God of order so they want to be pleasing in His sight.

Titus 3:1-2 says, "Put them in mind to be subject to principalities and powers, to obey magistrates, to be ready to every good work, To speak evil of no man, to be no brawlers, but gentle, shewing all meekness unto all men."

A person that's meek will not try to steal God's glory. They will remain in Him and God is able to use them in a powerful way.

Numbers 12:3 says, "(Now the man Moses was very meek, above all the men which were upon the face of the earth.)"

Because Moses was meek, God used him to do extraordinary miracles such as the parting of the red sea. Remain meek and watch the hand of the Lord raise you up.

CHAPTER THIRTY SIX
Temperance

Prophets need self-control or temperance. Temperance can also be defined as moderation or self-restraint in action, and abstinence.[18] Self-control means that we have control over our bodies and our minds. Actions and thoughts do not control us; we control what we think, and what we do. When we know something is wrong, but we do it anyway, we aren't controlled by the fruit of the Spirit. We have to be disciplined and not give into our carnal flesh. Living a fasted lifestyle helps prophets develop temperance.

Titus 2:12 says, "Teaching us that, denying ungodliness and worldly lusts, we should live soberly, righteously, and godly, in this present world;" Prophets need to deny ungodliness and worldly lusts.

Having self-control is a must. As you grow in God and acquire more knowledge of Him, adding temperance is key. Notice the steps in the following verses.

2 Peter 1:5-6 says, "And beside this, giving all diligence, add to your faith virtue; and to virtue knowledge; And to knowledge temperance; and to temperance patience; and to patience godliness;"

When you grow spiritually, more things are added. Whenever you lack self-control, there will be all kinds of doors open to the enemy.

Proverbs 25:28 says, "He that hath no rule over his own spirit is like a city that is broken down, and without walls."

As prophets, we have to ensure that every door to sin in our lives is closed. Years ago, I had an open door to the enemy. The devil was able to torment my mind. Since then, I've started to walk uprightly and closed the doors or portals to sin in my life, and the devil has no legal right to afflict me.

Jesus is a good example of a man who had temperance. He lived a sinless life.

Hebrews 4:15 says, "For we have not an high priest which cannot be touched with the feeling of our infirmities; but was in all points tempted like as we are, yet without sin."

He was able to overcome the lust of the flesh, the lust of the eyes, and the pride of life when He was tempted by Satan in the wilderness (Luke 4:1-13). He was submitted to God. We have to love God over everything to walk in victory.

James 4:7 says, "Submit yourselves, then, to God. Resist the devil, and he will flee from you."

There were plenty of times when I could've sinned against God but my flesh was dead to sin. I made up in my mind to never grieve the Holy Spirit. I developed a great love for Him and it kept me walking uprightly. As I yielded to the Holy Spirit, I always triumph over every stumbling block. Ask God to help you to develop temperance.

CHAPTER THIRTY SEVEN

Brokenness

Brokenness isn't always a bad thing. The world will teach you to be proud and lifted up. However, the word of God will teach you to be lowly. Brokenness is tamed, trained, or reduced to submission.[19] The hardships and the trials that I endured put me in a place of brokenness. I was trained by them and I had no other choice but to submit to God. Sometimes prophets are so stubborn that God has no other choice but to break them down. He has to do a great work in them and prune their flesh. After the breaking, then they are able to be used. God can then perform many signs and wonders through the broken vessel.

Jesus learned to obey God through his suffering.

Hebrews 5:8 says, "Though he were a Son, yet learned he obedience by the things which he suffered;"

When we are subdued totally and humbled, we are in a state of brokenness. When we are overwhelmed with sorrow, Godly sorrow, then we are in a state of brokenness. We begin to carry the burden of the Lord and care about what's on His heart. The prophet Jeremiah was constantly in a broken state.

Jeremiah 23:9 says, "Mine heart within me is broken because of the prophets; all my bones shake; I am like a drunken man, and like a man whom wine hath overcome, because of the Lord, and because of the words of his holiness."

Whenever we are broken, we are more sensitive to the needs of others. We can intercede for them more effectively because we understand the pain they might be experiencing. Whenever we are in a state of brokenness, we have a contrite heart. Our hearts are repentant before God.

Psalm 51:17 says, "The sacrifices of God are a broken spirit: a broken and a contrite heart, O God, thou wilt not despise."

King David was broken when he wrote Psalm 51. This is around the time when Nathan the prophet went to him, after he had sinned with Bathsheba. He was repenting before God. Being broken before God is a sacrifice and he will not despise you. You aren't weak but you are dependent on God. God is the strongest whenever you feel weak (2 Corinthians 12:9).

CHAPTER THIRTY EIGHT
Humility

Many prophets are prideful and arrogant. This should not be the case. God wants us to be humble. Humility is the same thing as lowly. Being humble is not having low self-esteem. For instance, many people feel like they have to lower themselves by saying, "I am nothing. I am no body" just to be humble. I disagree with this statement. You are someone. You are the child of the Most High God. You are wonderfully and fearfully made. Humility is replacing self-centeredness for Christ-centeredness. Humility is living in total freedom. Don't mind serving in the lowest or highest position that God decides to place you in. Humility is allowing God to defend you instead of you defending yourself.

Philippians 2:6-8 says, "Who, being in the form of God, thought it not robbery to be equal with God: But made himself of no reputation, and took upon him the form of a servant, and was made in the likeness of men: And being found in fashion as a man, he humbled himself, and became obedient unto death, even the death of the cross."

Jesus is the best model for humility. He humbled himself and became a servant. He washed his disciples' feet (John 13:1-17). Prophets need to be like Jesus and serve the body of Christ with the gifts on their lives. As we remain humble, God gives us grace.

James 4:6 says, "But he giveth more grace. Wherefore he saith, God resisteth the proud, but giveth grace unto the humble."

Whenever we are humble, we don't want anyone to worship us. We want the people to worship

Jesus. Always redirect the people's praises to God.

CHAPTER THIRTY NINE

Servants

Prophets are called to be servants. Beware of those prophets that want to be served but don't want to serve anyone. The gifts that God has placed inside of you are to serve the members in the body of Christ. Sometimes you have to sit under another man or woman of God for a season. Serving is a big responsibility. God is testing your faithfulness.

Luke 16:12 says, "And if ye have not been faithful in that which is another man's, who shall give you that which is your own?"

What exactly is serving? Servanthood is the state, condition, or quality of one who lives as a servant.[20] A servant is first of all one who is under submission to another. For Christians, this means submission to God first, and then submission to one another. To put it another way, servanthood is the condition or state of being a servant to others, of ministry to others, rather than the service of self. Serving takes giving of your time, effort, energy, talent, to accomplish the task no matter what. Jesus was a great servant. All day He performed miracles and at night He prayed (Mark 1:34-35).

Can you imagine ministering all day? By the end of the day, fatigue would set in. This is what Jesus sacrificed on a daily basis. When He saw the needs of the people, He did what He had to, to ensure every need was met.

Mark 10:45 says, "For even the Son of man came not to be ministered unto, but to minister, and to give his life a ransom for many."

Great leaders are the ones who are great at servanthood. Jesus had the right heart and He never abused the authority that was giving to him. He used his position to serve others. Some people use their position and misuse people instead of offering their services. Remember, the greatest is the servant of all.

Matthew 20:25-28 says, "But Jesus called them unto him, and said, Ye know that the princes of the Gentiles exercise dominion over them, and they that are great exercise authority upon them. But it shall not be so among you: but whosoever will be great among you, let him be your minister; And whosoever will be chief among you, let him be your servant: Even as the Son of man came not to be ministered unto, but to minister, and to give his life a ransom for many."

CHAPTER FORTY

Faith Filled

Faith in a prophet's life is vital. It's not optional but a requirement.

Hebrews 11:6 says, "But without faith it is impossible to please him: for he that cometh to God must believe that he is, and that he is a rewarder of them that diligently seek him."

It takes faith to prophesy (Romans 12:6), heal the sick (James 5:15), and raise the dead.

Acts 9:40 says, "But Peter put them all forth, and kneeled down, and prayed; and turning him to the body said, Tabitha, arise. And she opened her eyes: and when she saw Peter, she sat up."

Prophets have to trust God for everything. Elijah had to trust God to eat (1 Kings 17:6). Abraham had to trust God for the promise to be fulfilled (Genesis 12). On a daily basis, I have to trust God because He is my source for everything.

Jesus exhorted His disciples to "have the faith of God," and gave them authority to curse a fig tree or move a mountain. Jesus was hungry and came to a fig tree but it had no fruit. He cursed the tree and his disciples heard it (Mark 11:12-14). They went on to their destination and on their way back they passed by the same fig tree. The disciples remembered that Jesus cursed it and was amazed that the tree was withered at the roots. Jesus told his disciples to have faith in God and they will be able to do the same thing if they had faith. He told them that their faith could move mountains (Mark 11:20-24).

The faith of a prophet can produce manifestation of their spoken word. When Jesus said the fig tree would produce no more fruit, his words came to pass. Imagine how powerful your words will be when spoken in faith? Elijah prayed in faith about the rain and nature had no other choice but to obey his word.

1 Kings 17:1 says, "And Elijah the Tishbite, who was of the inhabitants of Gilead, said unto Ahab, As the Lord God of Israel liveth, before whom I stand, there shall not be dew nor rain these years, but according to my word."

CHAPTER FORTY ONE

Courageous

Prophets have to be courageous and not worry about what people think. You cann't be afraid to speak, "Thus saith the Lord?" Courageous can be defined as not being deterred by danger or pain; brave.[21] Synonyms of courageousness are brave, fearless, valiant, valorous, lionhearted, bold, daring, daredevil, audacious, undaunted, unflinching, unshrinking, unafraid, dauntless.[22] God told his prophets multiple times not to be afraid.

Isaiah 41:10 says, "Fear thou not; for I am with thee: be not dismayed; for I am thy God: I will strengthen thee; yea, I will help thee; yea, I will uphold thee with the right hand of my righteousness."

When God called Jeremiah, He dealt with his mouth. He placed His words in Jeremiah's mouth so he didn't have to be afraid to speak.

Jeremiah 1:9-10 says, "Then the Lord put forth his hand, and touched my mouth. And the Lord said unto me, Behold, I have put my words in thy mouth. See, I have this day set thee over the nations and over the kingdoms, to root out, and to pull down, and to destroy, and to throw down, to build, and to plant."

Elijah had to be courageous in 1 Kings 18 when he challenged the false prophets of Baal and Asherah. Jeremiah had to be courageous when people were wishing that he would trip and stumble. He knew that the Lord was with him and would avenge him (Jeremiah 20:10-11). We have to know that God is for us (Romans 8:31). God promised Jeremiah that He would strengthen him as a strong wall and that the attacks of the people who opposed him would not prosper against him. God told His prophet that He would deliver him out of trouble (Jeremiah 15:20-21).

God told Ezekiel that He was sending him to a group of rebellious people that wouldn't hear anything that he had to say. The group of people that Ezekiel had to prophesy had hard hearts toward God. However, God told this prophet that He was going to set his face like a flint, or the hardest rock, so he wouldn't walk in intimidation. He had no other choice but to be courageous (Ezekiel 3:4-10). No matter what adversity you face, be courageous because people are depending on your words!

CHAPTER FORTY TWO

Wise

Prophets have to walk in a level of wisdom. It's our jobs as prophets to have a good foundation in the word of God.

Proverbs 1:7 says, "The fear of the Lord is the beginning of knowledge: but fools despise wisdom and instruction."

To be wise is defined as having or showing experience, knowledge, and good judgment.[23]

Proverbs 1:5 says, "A wise man will hear, and will increase learning; and a man of understanding shall attain unto wise counsels:"

As prophets hear the word of God, their learning of the word will increase. This is why prophets should hang around with other prophets or another company of prophets so they can glean from each other and keep a strong prophetic atmosphere (1 Samuel 19:18–24; 2 Kings 2; 2 Kings 4:38–44).

Whenever we obey God, He is able to pour out His spirit upon us even more and give us more revelation.

Proverbs 1:23 says, "Turn you at my reproof: behold, I will pour out my spirit unto you, I will make known my words unto you."

The Lord wants us to acquire wisdom and he loves to give it to us (James 1:5).

Proverbs 2:2 says, "So that thou incline thine ear unto wisdom, and apply thine heart to understanding;"

The Lord will give wisdom to his people while protecting them in the process.

Proverbs 2:6-7 says, "For the Lord giveth wisdom: out of his mouth cometh knowledge and understanding. He layeth up sound wisdom for the righteous: he is a buckler to them that walk uprightly."

Whenever you are wise, people will seek you out. King Solomon was wise and many people sought him for counsel (1 Kings 3:16-28). The prophet Heman was very wise.

1 Kings 4:31 says, "For he was wiser than all men; than Ethan the Ezrahite, and Heman, and Chalcol, and Darda, the sons of Mahol: and his fame was in all nations round about."

The prophet Daniel was very wise and caused him to get promoted in the King's court.

Daniel 1:19-20 says, "And the king communed with them; and among them all was found none like Daniel, Hananiah, Mishael, and Azariah: therefore stood they before the king. And in all matters of wisdom and understanding, that the king enquired of them, he found them ten times better than all the magicians and astrologers that were in all his realm."

Whenever you walk uprightly, God will order your steps and give you wisdom. You don't have to settle and seek other sources such as divination. Seek the Holy Spirit. God will never lead you astray!

CHAPTER FORTY THREE

Spirit Led

Prophets need to make sure that they are spirit led. I made mistakes before and did things that God didn't tell me to do. I was so zealous that I did things out of season and became frustrated. We have to make sure that God is in something so he can prosper it and we walk in total obedience. We need to walk in the spirit by crucifying our flesh and put our agenda down and pick up God's agenda.

Galatians 5:24-25 says, "And they that are Christ's have crucified the flesh with the affections and lusts. If we live in the Spirit, let us also walk in the Spirit."

We are called the sons of God when we follow after His spirit.

Romans 8:14 says, "For as many as are led by the Spirit of God, they are the sons of God."

God will lead us on the right path in life.

Psalm 143:10 says, "Teach me to do thy will; for thou art my God: thy spirit is good; lead me into the land of uprightness."

Many prophets have started out on the right path but lost their way along their way because they allowed greed, lust, perversion, and other sins to set in. They started spending less time with God and weren't able to discern that His presence wasn't present.

The Holy Spirit wants to guide us and show us the way.

John 16:13 says, "Howbeit when he, the Spirit of truth, is come, he will guide you into all truth: for he shall not speak of himself; but whatsoever he shall hear, that shall he speak: and he will shew you things to come."

Many people need direction in life. When we submit to the Holy Spirit, he will show us the way.

Isaiah 30:21 says, "And thine ears shall hear a word behind thee, saying, This is the way, walk ye in it, when ye turn to the right hand, and when ye turn to the left."

God will place us where He wants us at certain times and seasons. I was in a wilderness season for three years. That was my season of training and when I got called as a prophet. I prayed to God one day before I moved across the country. I said, "Lord, I want to be close to you." I forgot about that prayer. Shortly after, my life was turned upside, and I got close to God. I was about to leave the state of Colorado one day but when I prayed about it, the Lord told me to stay. The trial got worse, but I received an anointing on my life. I was being led by the Holy Spirit. Jesus was led by the Holy Spirit into the wilderness.

Luke 4:1 says, "And Jesus being full of the Holy Ghost returned from Jordan, and was led by the Spirit into the wilderness."

The Spirit gave the church at Antioch instructions.

Acts 13:2 says, "As they ministered to the Lord, and fasted, the Holy Ghost said, Separate me Barnabas and Saul for the work whereunto I have called them."

The Holy Spirit led Philip to minister to an Ethiopian Eunich. He got saved and baptized.

Acts 8:29 says, "Then the Spirit said unto Philip, Go near, and join thyself to this chariot."

Imagine how effective you will be when you are spirit led?

CHAPTER FORTY FOUR

Obedient to God

Prophets need to follow the voice of the Lord regardless of how uncomfortable it is. How can God trust you when you walk in disobedience?

Psalm 119:60 says, "I made haste, and delayed not to keep thy commandments."

Once I had to give words to a group of leaders and it was very uncomfortable. God told me to do it and I did it. God told His prophet Jeremiah to obey His voice.

Jeremiah 7:23 says, "But this thing commanded I them, saying, Obey my voice, and I will be your God, and ye shall be my people: and walk ye in all the ways that I have commanded you, that it may be well unto you."

Amos was obedient to his called. He was watching his flock of sheep one day and God told him to go prophesy. He stopped what he was doing and spoke the word of the Lord.

Amos 7:15 says, "And the Lord took me as I followed the flock, and the Lord said unto me, Go, prophesy unto my people Israel."

Whenever we disobey God, the consequences can be fatal. This is what happen in 1 Kings 13. A young prophet disobeyed God, and it caused him his life. God told him not to go to anyone's house and not to eat anything. An old prophet tricked him and he went to his house and ate. The word of the Lord came and when the prophet left that house, a lion killed him. Take the time and walk in total obedience to God. I tell countless testimonies of my obedience to God in one of my books, "Obedience Is Key."

Prophets have to obey God on what to speak. They don't need to add anything more or less to the word of the Lord. We have to have wisdom and be able to discern when to stop talking.

Deuteronomy 18:18 says, "I will raise them up a Prophet from among their brethren, like unto thee, and will put my words in his mouth; and he shall speak unto them all that I shall command him."

There are blessing associated with obedience. We are called to keep his commandments.

1 Kings 2:3 says, "And keep the charge of the Lord thy God, to walk in his ways, to keep his statutes, and his commandments, and his judgments, and his testimonies, as it is written in the law of Moses, that thou mayest prosper in all that thou doest, and whithersoever thou turnest thyself:"

CHAPTER FORTY FIVE

Integrity

Prophets need to have integrity. Integrity can be defined as the quality of being honest and having strong moral principles; moral uprightness.[24] There are many people who lack integrity. They are corrupted and don't care about God or His people. They will do anything to get ahead and lack the standards of the word of God and holiness. This shouldn't be so. Many churches are corrupted. Preachers are fornicating with the members. Preachers are trying to justify certain sins and abominations and twist the scriptures.

Proverbs 11:3 says, "The integrity of the upright shall guide them: but the perverseness of transgressors shall destroy them."

If the word of God says it is wrong, then it's wrong. There is no gray area between: either its black or white. We may stumble at times but we need to be repenting before God just like David did.

1 Kings 9:4-5 says, "And if thou wilt walk before me, as David thy father walked, in integrity of heart, and in uprightness, to do according to all that I have commanded thee, and wilt keep my statutes and my judgments: Then I will establish the throne of thy kingdom upon Israel for ever, as I promised to David thy father, saying, There shall not fail thee a man upon the throne of Israel."

Enoch had so much integrity that he walked with God.

Genesis 5:24 says, "And Enoch walked with God: and he was not; for God took him."

Don't grieve the Holy Spirit. Become His friend and walk in integrity.

CHAPTER FORTY SIX

Compassion

Prophets need to have compassion on God's people. Compassion can be defined as sympathetic pity and concern for the sufferings or misfortunes of others.[25] The reason why many prophets go through some horrible trials is to gain compassion. Because I was almost homeless several times, I love to feed the poor. I make time to serve at various food banks. Because I went through a devastating time of a failed marriage, I have sympathy of single parents and people believing God for restoration of their marriages.

We are called to have a heart of compassion or have bowels of mercy.

Colossians 3:12-13 says, "Put on therefore, as the elect of God, holy and beloved, bowels of mercies, kindness, humbleness of mind, meekness, longsuffering; Forbearing one another, and forgiving one another, if any man have a quarrel against any: even as Christ forgave you, so also do ye."

This is probably why biblical prophets shed more tears than the priest and the kings, because compassion was at the heart of their ministry.

Jeremiah was a compassionate prophet or weeping prophet. He often wept over the words that the Lord gave him to speak.

Jeremiah 8:21-9:1 says, "For the hurt of the daughter of my people am I hurt; I am black; astonishment hath taken hold on me. Is there no balm in Gilead; is there no physician there? why then is not the health of the daughter of my people recovered? Oh that my head were waters, and mine eyes a fountain of tears, that I might weep day and night for the slain of the daughter of my people!"

Jesus even had compassion on people. He performed one of the greatest miracles when He feed the multitude (Mark 6:30-44).

Mark 6:34 says, "And Jesus, when he came out, saw much people, and was moved with compassion toward them, because they were as sheep not having a shepherd: and he began to teach them many things."

CHAPTER FORTY SEVEN

Commitment

Prophets can't quit when it gets hard. I wanted to walk away from everything before. I was severely depressed and prayed to die because the trials were so intense. At that time, Jesus was the only thing that gave me hope and fulfillment. Even way after that dark moments, walking in my call gives me a sense of achievement. I am now ready to take on any setbacks that come my way to challenge me. I am committed to God. Every time I do something great for God, the warfare comes. I know I am exactly where God wants me. I always come out victoriously.

Prophets must meet opposition with tenacity. We have to be totally committed to God's purpose. Once called, a prophet must be totally loyal to their ministry and God. They cannot swerve to the left or the right.

Luke 9:62 says, "And Jesus said unto him, No man, having put his hand to the plough, and looking back, is fit for the kingdom of God."

Loyalty to God must never be shaken, no matter the circumstances. Ezekiel was committed to God. After he had a heavenly encounter (Ezekiel 1), he received his call. Initially, anger and bitterness crept in but the Lord dealt with him (Ezekiel 3:14). He served his assignment regardless of the difficulties.

Prophets have to be task focused. There were times when my computer crashed while I was writing books. Once, someone put a virus on my laptop and it wiped out all my files for the books that I was writing. However, the Lord blessed me to get it all back. I had my mind set on the task and was determined to finish my assignment. Sometimes prophets have to suffer because their calling will cost them everything. Jeremiah understood that he could let nothing stop him from fulfilling his calling. He wasn't allowed to marry or have children.

Jeremiah 16:2 says, "Thou shalt not take thee a wife, neither shalt thou have sons or daughters in this place."

When Jeremiah felt discouraged and didn't want to prophesy anymore, he felt the fire of the Lord in his bones. He then continued in his calling (Jeremiah 20:7-10). Will you quit when it gets hard or will you stick it out?

CHAPTER FORTY EIGHT

Righteousness

Prophets have to practice righteousness. When I got the revelation of righteousness, it changed my life. I received a scepter of righteousness in the spirit realm. I wrote about my encounter with God in my book, "In Right Standing." Righteousness means to be in right standing with God. Our ways need to please God. Our heart needs to be pure in His sight. Christ died for us to make us righteous (Romans 5:17-18). Why nail Him back on the cross by your wicked ways? This is one reason why we can see a pattern in the word of God when His prophets cry out against injustice and unrighteousness.

David cried out when he saw the wicked prospering and getting away with things (Psalm 24; 37). Habakkuk cried out (Habakkuk 1). This is why prophets are grieved when they see sin in the church. Zechariah had a vision of the high priest. His vision was prophetic of what Jesus did for us. He took off filthy garments and put on clean garments. It didn't matter what the devil tried to accuse him with. Jesus came to remove the inequities. He was the high priest (Zechariah 3: 1-10). Bring Glory to God and promote righteousness. Set a standard in the prophetic ministry.

CHAPTER FORTY NINE

Surrendered

Prophets have to be surrendered to God. Surrendered means submission or yielding.[26] We have to be abided in God to yield fruit and to allow His will to be done in our lives (John 15:1-7). After God dealt with me and got the stubbornness and rebellion out of me, I surrendered everything to him. I gave up my aspirations of becoming a medical doctor to say yes to the call on my life. I stopped compromising my walk with him and got serious with him. I lost my life and gained a new one in him. I let go of the past. If we try to save our life, we will lose it. If we let go of our life, we will find it.

Matthew 16:25 says, "For whosoever will save his life shall lose it: and whosoever will lose his life for my sake shall find it."

We must give to get. Letting go is the way to receive. We must sow to reap (Galatians 6:7). Apostle Paul showed how surrendered he was to God when he didn't go to Asia to spread the gospel. He wanted to go there but the Holy Spirit forbid him and the saints that were with him.

Acts 16:6 says, "They passed through the Phrygian and Galatian region, having been forbidden by the Holy Spirit to speak the word in Asia;"

What are you willing to give up for God in order to fulfil your assignment?

About The Author

Kimberly Moses started off her ministry as Kimberly Hargraves. She is a highly sought after prophetic voice, Intercessor and a prolific author. There is no doubt that she has a global mandate on her life to serve the nations of the world by spreading the Gospel of JesusChrist. She has a quickly expanding worldwide healing and deliveranceministry. Kimberly Moses wears many hats to fulfill the call God has placed on her life as an entrepreneur over several businesses including her own personal brand Rejoice Essentials which promotes the Gospel of Jesus Christ. This brand includes a magazine and anointing oils. She also serves as a life coach and mentor to many women. She is married to Tron and also the loving mother of two wonderful children. Kimberly has dedicated her life to the work of ministry and to serve others under the call God has placed over her life.

Kimberly currently resides in South Carolina. She is a very anointed woman of God who signs, miracles and wonders follow. The miraculous and incessant testimonies attributed to her ministry are incalculable, with many reporting physical and mental healing, financial breakthroughs, debt cancellations and other favorable outcomes. She is known across the globe as a servant who truly labors on behalf of God's people through intercession. God blessed her to start her ministry to help encourage others. God used her pain to reveal her writing ability and to do his work. God blessed her to write about life experiences and give a message of hope to others with broken hearts.

She is the author of The Following:

"Overcoming Difficult Life Experiences with Scriptures and

Prayers"

"Overcoming Emotions with Prayers"

"Daily Prayers That Bring Changes"

"In Right Standing,"

"Obedience Is Key,"

"Prayers That Break The Yoke Of The Enemy: A Book Of

Declarations,"

"Prayers That Demolish Demonic Strongholds: A Book Of

Declarations,"

"Work Smarter. Not Harder. A Book Of Declarations For The Workforce,"

"Set The Captives Free: A Book Of Deliverance."

"Pray More Challenge"

"Empowering The New Me: Fifty Tips To Becoming A Godly Woman"

"Walk By Faith: A Daily Devotional"

"School Of The Prophets: A Curriculum For Success"

"Conquering The Mind: A Daily Devotional"

"8 Keys To Accessing The Supernatural"

You can find more about Kimberly at

www.prophetessk.org. Follow Kimberly on Facebook at

https://www.facebook.com/seerprophetesskimberlyhargraves/.

Follow Kimberly on Twitter and periscope @ SeerProphetessK.

References

1. "Enhance." Merriam-Webster.com. Merriam-Webster, n.d. Web. 5 Nov. 2017.
2. " What is prophetic ministry?" (n.d.). Retrieved June 10, 2017 from https://www.gotquestions.org/prophetic-ministry.html
3. rhema. (n.d.). Dictionary.com's 21st Century Lexicon. Retrieved June 21, 2017 from Dictionary.com website http://www.dictionary.com/browse/rhema
4. Eckhardt, J. (2009). God Still Speaks. Lake Mary, Florida: Charisma House.
5. Evans, R. L. (2014) The Prophetic Mantle: The Gift of Prophecy and Prophetic Operations in the Church Today. Abundant Truth Publishing on Smashwords
6. vehicle. (n.d.). Roget's 21st Century Thesaurus, Third Edition. Retrieved June 28, 2017 from Thesaurus.com website http://www.thesaurus.com/browse/vehicles?s=t
7. Hargraves, K (2017). Activating The Voice Of God In Your Life. Retrieved June 28, 2017

from Rejoice Essential Magazine. https://issuu.com/rejoiceessentialmagazine/docs/january_rejoice_essential_2017

8. Coxe, John Redman (1808-01-01). The Philadelphia Medical Dictionary: Containing a Concise Explanation of All the Terms Used in Medicine, Surgery, Pharmacy, Botany, Natural History, Chymistry, and Materia Medica. Thomas Dobson; Thomas and George Palmer, printers.

9. reaffirmation. (n.d.). Dictionary.com Unabridged. Retrieved July 18, 2017 from Dictionary.com website http://www.dictionary.com/browse/reaffirmation

10. "Proxy." Merriam-Webster.com. Merriam-Webster, n.d. Web. 27 July 2017.

11. parable. (n.d.). Dictionary.com Unabridged. Retrieved July 27, 2017 from Dictionary.com website http://www.dictionary.com/browse/parable

12. "Action." Merriam-Webster.com. Merriam-Webster, n.d. Web. 27 July 2017.

13. "Characteristic." Merriam-Webster.com. Merriam-Webster, n.d. Web. 27 Oct. 2017.

14. characteristic. (n.d.). Roget's 21st Century Thesaurus, Third Edition. Retrieved October 27,

2017 from Thesaurus.com website http://www.thesaurus.com/browse/characteristic

15. "Gentle." Merriam-Webster.com. Merriam-Webster, n.d. Web. 29 Oct. 2017.

16. "Goodness." Merriam-Webster.com. Merriam-Webster, n.d. Web. 29 Oct. 2017.

17. meekness. (n.d.). Dictionary.com Unabridged. Retrieved November 3, 2017 from Dictionary.com website http://www.dictionary.com/browse/meekness

18. temperance. (n.d.). Dictionary.com Unabridged. Retrieved November 3, 2017 from Dictionary.com website http://www.dictionary.com/browse/temperance

19. brokenness. (n.d.). Dictionary.com Unabridged. Retrieved November 3, 2017 from Dictionary.com website http://www.dictionary.com/browse/brokenness

20. Mark #8: The Heart of a Servant. Accessed November 4, 2017 from https://bible.org/seriespage/mark-8-heart-servant

21. Courageous. (n.d.). Dictionary.com Unabridged. Retrieved November 5, 2017 from Dictionary.com website http://www.dictionary.com/browse/courageous

22. courageous. (n.d.). Roget's 21st Century Thesaurus, Third Edition. Retrieved November 5, 2017, from Thesaurus.com website http://www.thesaurus.com/browse/courageous

23. wise. (n.d.). Dictionary.com Unabridged. Retrieved November 5, 2017 from Dictionary.com website http://www.dictionary.com/browse/wise

24. integrity. (n.d.). Dictionary.com Unabridged. Retrieved November 5, 2017 from Dictionary.com website http://www.dictionary.com/browse/integrity

25. compassion. (n.d.). Dictionary.com Unabridged. Retrieved November 5, 2017 from Dictionary.com website http://www.dictionary.com/browse/compassion

26. surrender. (n.d.). Dictionary.com Unabridged. Retrieved November 5, 2017 from Dictionary.com website http://www.dictionary.com/browse/surrender

Index

A

Amos, 3, 82
abominations, 62, 205
accountable, 65
Abraham, 162
administration, 54, 109
Ahab, King, 128
Amos, 203
angels, 47, 101–2, 105, 134, 136, 138
anointing, 171
Antioch, 52, 96
Apostle Peter, 99, 114
apostles, 53–54, 166
Asaph, 12
assignment, 169, 171, 213, 217
authorities, 33, 187

B

Baruch, 111–12
believing, 155–56
bless, 41, 106, 134, 137, 158

body of Christ, 27, 50–52, 183
brokenness, 66, 179-80, 223

C

captives, 114, 165
characteristics, 37, 144, 222
charity, 43, 59, 150
children, 104, 147, 166–67, 170, 213, 218
churches, 30–33, 42, 47, 52, 74, 96, 215
commandments, 105, 134, 204
compassion, 43, 65, 208–10
  bowels of, 153
confirmation, 93, 95
confusion, 31–32, 42
counsel, 41, 61, 147
countenance, 17, 68
courageous, 191–93

D

Daniel, 102–3, 114–15, 130, 132, 160, 196
David, King, 181
deliverance, 108
destruction, 37
devil, 147, 165, 170, 177

discern, 144, 204
disciples, 108, 118, 124, 183, 189
division, 33, 52, 62
dreams, 90–91, 94, 98–99, 102–3, 132
dreams, 94, 98, 102

E

edification, 28
edifying, 59, 61
Effective ministry, 42
Elijah, 87, 146, 190, 192
enemies, 10–11, 15, 140, 151, 176
Enoch, 206
Ethiopian Eunuch, 86
excellence, 168
expectation, 154
Ezekiel, 21–22, 92, 102, 110, 127, 193, 212

F

faith, 15–17, 38–39, 59, 90, 107–8, 130, 150, 172, 188–90
fasted lifestyle, 7–8
fasting, 7, 84
faithfulness, 170–71

fruit, 69, 120–21, 145–46, 159, 167, 189
fulfillment, 211
functions, 74

G

gentleness, 164, 166
gifts, 17, 27–28, 38, 46, 59, 67–68, 109, 132, 145, 147, 168
gossip, 61–62
grace, 38, 109, 183
guidance, 41, 50, 142
guide, 50, 57, 200, 206

H

Habakkuk, 9, 102, 160, 215
haughty spirit, 37
heaven, 60, 103, 109, 118, 132
holiness, 63–64, 180
holy lifestyle, 63
Holy Spirit, 58, 84–85, 217
Humility, 37, 41, 182–83

I

instructions, 8–9, 141, 194

integrity, 205–7
intercedes, 52–53, 181
intercessors, 67
Isaiah, 113, 192, 200

J

Jeremiah, 91, 111, 113–14, 128, 171, 180, 192, 203, 209, 213
Jesus, 7, 9, 43–44, 108–9, 118–19, 121–23, 150–51, 177, 180, 183–84, 186–87, 189–90, 210, 212, 215
Jezebel, 146
joy, 34, 154–56, 159
Judah, 111
judgments, 105, 113, 168, 204, 206

K

kingdom, 109, 113, 118, 161, 192, 212
knowledge, 26, 38, 59, 72, 108, 176, 194

L

leaders, 30, 33, 41
light, 109, 142, 152, 167

longsuffering, 37, 160–61, 209
love, 28, 37, 43–44, 58–59, 66, 68–69, 126, 149–52, 172, 208
lusts, worldly, 176

M

manifestation, 74
marriage, 104, 126, 208
marrow, 24, 140
marvelous sight, 102
meditation, 12, 25
meekness, 37, 62, 161, 165, 172–73, 209
mercies, 105, 132, 161, 209
Messiah, 141
ministry, 26–27, 32, 63, 65, 84, 209, 218
minstrel, 13
miracles, 63, 66
Miriam, 90
misfortunes, 208
mountains, 59, 87, 189
mouth, 18, 20, 23–25, 61, 90–91, 95–96, 108, 111, 118, 192, 204

N

Nathan, 118
Nebuchadnezzar, King, 103

O

offices, five-fold, 31, 50, 52, 54

P

pain, 65, 181, 191
parables, 117–19, 121
pastors, 51–52, 153
patience, 161–62, 172
peace, 31–32, 42, 113, 156–59
Pentecost, 99
perception, 104
perseverance, 67
perverseness, 206
Peter, 3, 41, 48, 63, 65, 89, 141, 155, 176, 189
prayer, 9, 18, 22, 56, 66–67, 129, 131, 133, 157, 160, 162
Pride, 37
priests, 114, 136
principalities, 173
promises, 155, 162
prophetic flow, 82

prophetic visions, 101
prophetic word, 136
prophesy, 11, 15–16, 31–32, 35–36, 38, 43, 48, 89, 99, 131, 138, 146, 150–51, 193, 203
prophetic action, 125–26, 128
prophetic anointing, 17, 153
prophetic gift, 28
prophetic message, 125, 128, 136
prophetic office, 28, 51
Prophetic Protocol, 30, 36
prophetic revelation, 3
prophetic training, 3
Prophetic Vehicles, 72
prophets, 16–17, 32, 40–43, 47–48, 50–55, 66–67, 89–92, 113–14, 118–19, 145–47, 154–55, 160–61, 169, 175–76, 194–95
prophet's DNA, 9

R

Reaffirmation, 95
revelation, 2, 27, 32, 34, 47, 52, 58, 78, 114, 129, 139, 141, 145, 170, 195
righteousness, 2, 23, 76, 141, 167, 172, 192, 214

S

sacrifices, 151, 171, 181
Samuel, 105
secrets, 109, 118, 132
self-control, 175–76
servants, 92, 146, 165, 183, 185–87
sexual immorality, 147
shield, 100, 142
Silas, 96
souls, 24, 33–34, 53, 130, 140, 166, 173
spiritual milk, 28, 120
stewards, 169
strength, 79, 101, 134, 142, 155, 158–59, 171
submission, 34, 40, 179
supplication, 67, 157

T

tarry, 116, 130
teachers, 52
temperance, 175, 177–78
testimonies, 203–4
Timothy, 14, 141, 165, 172
Titus, 62, 173, 176
tongues, 10, 45, 62

tribulation, 67, 162, 169–70

U

ungodliness, 176

V

vessel, 33
visions, 33, 91, 98–103, 116, 130, 138, 215
voice, 7, 10, 35, 77–81, 87, 100, 106, 134, 202–3

W

whoredoms, 170
wilderness, 78, 201
worship, 12–13, 30, 46–47, 183

Y

yoke, 57, 173

Z

Zechariah, 102, 137–38, 215

www.ingramcontent.com/pod-product-compliance
Lightning Source LLC
Chambersburg PA
CBHW071606080526
44588CB00010B/1031